Dear Meg,
May the good Lord
Bless You... _____ love,

-13

Healing Prayer on Holy Ground is a riveting account of suffering, near-death experiences, healings, and discovering God in the context of illness and trauma. The Sheehans encourage us to believe that healing miracles that occurred in apostolic times can and do happen today. The book challenges us to lay hold, through prayer, of the power of the gospel for the healing of disease, extension of the kingdom, and the glory of the Creator and Redeemer God. Here is a truly encouraging and life-affirming read.

—BRUCE DEMAREST, PHD
PROFESSOR OF CHRISTIAN FORMATION
DENVER SEMINARY, LITTLETON, COLORADO

On Sunday morning, December 17, 2006, I was driving to church when a crushing pain seized my chest. I knew instantly what was happening and turned to my wife, Ellen, saying, "Sweetheart, I am having a heart attack. Let's go home and get some nitroglycerin." "No," she replied, "we're going to the hospital and get you a doctor."

Ellen slipped behind the wheel, and in record time we pulled up to the Swedish Hospital Emergency Room, where three people were waiting for me at the door. Seconds later, laying on a gurney with a nitro drip in my arm; sensors and wires plugged into my arms, legs, and chest; staring up into a blinding overhead light; still in great pain; I met a remarkable man, Dr. Mark Sheehan, an eminent cardiologist.

Dr. Sheehan had returned from church and had come to the hospital on Sunday morning to see another patient. It was my good fortune—a divine appointment?—that he was on hand at what was for me a life-or-death moment. With cool professional poise, "Doc" opened me up, inserted a catheter in my groin and threaded a video camera through a blood vessel into my heart so he could see what had caused my heart attack. As you can imagine, I also watched the video monitor with considerable interest.

It only took a moment for Dr. Sheehan to determine that a crucial blood vessel was shut down and that surgery was the only answer. Thanks to his timely and professional skill, my life was saved and, happily, multiple bypass surgery restored me to full health without lasting damage to my heart.

Since then I've been seeing Dr. Sheehan professionally, and on Sunday mornings at Cherry Hills Community Church. In addition to being a noted physician and cardiologist, I have learned that he is a medical missionary and a great man of God. But only recently have I discovered that God has given Dr. Mark Sheehan another gift—writing.

Most doctors are not good writers. This should be no surprise since most writers can't diagnose and treat illness. Both medicine and writing are demanding professional disciplines and not many are able to master either one, let alone both. Only a handful of physicians—St. Luke being the most notable example—can really tell a story with clarity and compelling power. Mark Sheehan is such a person.

In the book you are about to read, you'll be fascinated to learn a little of Mark's early life as one of "seven wild and wayward sons…" who "boxed, clawed, and…filled the house with pent-up testosterone." You'll learn about how Mark met his wife, Linda, their life together, and the wonderful story of how he came to Christ.

You'll meet Kasey who was "clinically dead" but came back to life with a remarkable story to tell. You'll learn why only about half of doctors believe in God, but 95 percent of nurses do. You will encounter a penetrating critique of the educational system that turns scientists against God and much more. But the main point of this extraordinary narrative is prayer—what it is, the remarkable healing power of prayer, and the documented results of doctors, nurses, patients, and families who pray.

This is a wonderful book. Turn off your cell phone and settle in for a great read.

—Senator Bill Armstrong
President of Colorado Christian University
Denver, Colorado

HEALING
PRAYER

ON HOLY
GROUND

MARK W. SHEEHAN, M.D., with CHRIS SHEEHAN

CREATION
HOUSE
A STRANG COMPANY

HEALING PRAYER ON HOLY GROUND by Mark W. Sheehan, MD, with Chris Sheehan
Published by Creation House
A Strang Company
600 Rinehart Road
Lake Mary, Florida 32746
www.strangbookgroup.com

Unless otherwise noted, all Scripture quotations are from the Holy Bible, New International Version of the Bible. Copyright © 1973, 1978, 1984, International Bible Society. Used by permission.

Design Director: Bill Johnson
Cover design by Justin Evans

Library of Congress Control Number: 2010920472
International Standard Book Number: 978-1-61638-151-6
(paperback)

First Edition

10 11 12 13 14 — 9 8 7 6 5 4 3 2 1
Printed in the United States of America

CONTENTS

PART 1

PERSONAL TRANSFORMATION

CHAPTER 1

TOUCHED BY GOD'S GRACE

"For I know the plans I have for you," declares the Lord, "plans to prosper you and not to harm you, plans to give you hope and a future. Then you will call upon me and come and pray to me, and I will listen to you. You will seek me and find me when you seek me with all your heart."

—JEREMIAH 29:11–13

A T THE AGE of thirty-five, Kasey had severe premature lung disease. Her lung capacity was less than half of a normal person's, and her ability to expel air from her lungs was only 25 percent of a normal person's. There was little use in trying to blow up balloons on birthdays. On Christmas day, after exchanging gifts with her husband and young son, she felt ill and told her husband to drive her to the hospital. For many people with her condition, the act of breathing can be exhausting and labored work for hours at a time. Kasey described it as having to "hyperventilate" in order to get the oxygen she needed. For six days she propped herself up crossed-legged in bed, holding on to a nearby table for support. She was unable to rest, unable to sleep, and unable to eat, focusing only on her breathing.

Kasey told a medical worker twice that she felt like she was going into a respiratory arrest and asked the worker to call her doctor. The therapist assured her both times that she was going to be fine. Finally, in what Kasey later described as a "not-too-pleasant voice," she said: "Read my lips: I'm going into arrest." And with that, her heart stopped beating, and her lungs stopped working; she was then "clinically dead."

Meanwhile, at 4:45 p.m. that day, I was almost in vacation mode. In 15 minutes our office was going to refer new patients to another doctor. I was planning to leave the next day on a Caribbean cruise with my family. Suddenly I was alerted to Kasey's situation. When I arrived at her side she was on life support. Her skin was blue, her cardiac output was around 20 percent of normal, and the pressure in her lungs was over two times as high as normal. Prior to my arrival, electrical countershocks had been applied repeatedly in an attempt to restart her heart.

I tried to increase her blood pressure by inserting an intra-aortic balloon catheter inside her femoral artery. After four hours of working on her I'd gotten nowhere. I went into the waiting room and told her husband that I didn't think she would make it.

Kasey wavered for three days between life and death. While unconscious, she had a near-death experience and out of body experience, which she later claimed in a thorough testimony were far more vivid than normal dreams. During one vision, she saw what seemed like the City of God. She saw 12 distinct gates around this city, each of which seemed made of a single pearl. She saw 12 distinct foundations of differing colors. Though she had never read the last book of the Bible, which describes the City of God in detail, she found that her testimony matched the Bible's account to an astonishing degree.

Furthermore, Kasey was able to recount, word for word, conversations that had taken place around her body between nurses and doctors. She later shared with me her written testimony of what had happened in her immediate physical surroundings while she had been unconscious. She described both what I had been wearing and also precise procedures I had performed. I would not have believed it was possible for her to be aware of such things, but she was not wrong about a single detail.

In another vision, she had even seen the exact car model of one of her doctors and the exact route he took to leave his home and arrive at the hospital, though she had no idea previously where he lived or what type of car he owned. He was stunned when Kasey shared these details with him, and he had no explanation.

Additionally, while unconscious Kasey had heard four distinct voices praying and speaking to each other. One of these voices had boomed: "And the gates of darkness shall not prevail!" After she recovered, Kasey found that those four people were part of one of her church's prayer groups, which they had assembled on her behalf. Though they met many miles from the hospital, her account of their words matched up exactly with what they had said.

Kasey also witnessed what she later believed was the presence of God during her near-death experience, as have so many other people who have gone through near-death experiences. She came away from her ordeal convinced that the power of prayer had played a part in her recovery, that God had a plan for her life, and that heaven was a reality. Her story, and others I will recount, cannot be explained by logic or dismissed as a matter of coincidence. The stories are both too compelling and too common. Similar near-death experiences have been chronicled by such best-selling authors as

Larry Dossey and Raymond Moody Jr. I will share the rest of Kasey's inspiring story in a later chapter.

God's presence is nowhere more active, unmistakable, or comforting than in the lives of sick and dying patients. This book deals primarily with the transformative grace of that presence, as well as the healing power of prayer in the context of medicine. I will share examples from my own patient interactions and from those of other doctors. I will reveal how my own faith has changed the way I live my life, specifically in the way I practice clinical medicine as a cardiologist. Some episodes, such as Kasey's story, concern near-death experiences and how these experiences impacted everyone involved. I want to lift peoples' hopes with the certainty that God truly has a plan for all of us and that prayer is no empty gesture but the means by which we communicate with God and understand His plan for our lives.

I will also discuss the role of the caring profession, specifically as it applies to medicine, patient advocacy, and nursing. Kasey later said that one of the things she was most thankful for was that she could find Christian doctors who wouldn't be dismissive of her spiritual beliefs and hopes and with whom she could share more than just accounts of her latest symptoms. The health care profession is not often comfortable with talk of the healing power of prayer or divine healing. Doctors in general believe in God at much lower levels than the overall population, and many seem downright indifferent or dismissive of the subject. But this book will argue that an overwhelming percentage of patients believe in prayer, take great hope from God, and prefer health care workers to be sensitive to spiritual needs.

I believe *the room of a dying patient is holy ground* in which I should almost remove my shoes. The conversations, the anguish, the confessions, the tears, the acceptance, the peace, and the prayers are uniquely memorable and healing. My belief in the power of prayer in particular has been consistently strengthened by what I've seen, which is partly why I've titled this book *Healing Prayer on Holy Ground*. It has truly been a privilege to be a witness and humble practitioner alongside my patients. Regardless of a patient's specific beliefs, I believe God is present. Thus, I am aiming this book at people from all faiths, as well as those without faith.

My concept of faith is well described in Hebrews 11:1-2. Verse 1 states, "Now faith is being sure of what we hope for and certain of what we do not see." In verse 6 the writer goes on: "And without faith it is impossible to please God, because anyone who comes to him must believe that he exists and that he rewards those who earnestly seek him." If any situation makes people seek God, it is being faced with one's mortality. As the familiar cliché goes, "There are no atheists in a foxhole." And the dying room is a foxhole of sorts, where there may be a noticeable shortage of people without some faith. For many, faith is renewed in their lives to unprecedented levels, and for some, faith is present for the first time. These miracles, I believe, are a result of God's grace. By *grace* I mean the unmerited benevolence of God. The presence of a strong faith is usually associated with the kind of peaceful death most people hope for, because they know they are going to a better place where they will have no pain.

My personal walk and experience with prayer and faith is not unique, but it nevertheless laid the foundation for the way I now view the dying room. I was raised the second of seven wild and wayward sons by two parents who used everything but the National Guard to keep us in line. We boxed, we clawed, and we filled the house with plenty of pent-up testosterone. Among the crises my parents faced: sons accidentally falling from cupboards and impaling themselves on meat hooks, running through glass doors, having arrows fired into their throats, getting in motorcycle accidents, needing to be bailed out of jail, and more.

Around the dinner table my brothers and I often behaved more like starving hyenas than respectable young men. This was never more evident than the first time I brought my future wife, Linda, over for dinner. We had a lazy susan in the middle of the table where the food was laid out so that our family could spin it around to get what they wanted. Once the food was set down my family reached out with forks and grabbed what they wanted. Linda came from a family where people said, "Please pass the peas," and "Thank you very much," and she wasn't used to this. When we were finished my mother asked Linda how she liked the food. Linda replied that she hadn't received any. Everyone was so intent on eating that no one had noticed. Her fork was not fast enough.

We weren't always what the neighbors called the "most Christian of boys," but that wasn't because our parents and their parents in turn didn't take Christianity seriously. My father, raised Catholic, was a hard-working engineer who devoted his life to raising us. My mother was a Presbyterian who kept us in line only with great patience and inexhaustible humor. My uncle, John Sheehan, was a Roman Catholic Basilian priest. My father's great aunt, Sister Agatha, was a librarian of the Incarnate Word Convent in Houston, Texas. My grandmother was raised as a Christian Scientist and had a strong faith. I consider her a major prayer warrior. She had a major impact on my life and encouraged me to pursue my dreams and have the confidence and faith to go where God was leading me.

At age 11 I was very involved in the Boy Scouts and eventually earned my Eagle Scout Award. The Boy Scouts placed great importance on giving back to society. This struck a chord with me and still does, and at the time it influenced my career path. I remember being impressed by President Kennedy's line: "Ask not what your country can do for you; ask what you can do for your country." In a 2002 speech at Notre Dame University, President George W. Bush suggested that part of the responsibility in being an American is serving "something greater than yourself."[1] As examples of this spirit, he cited teachers as well as the Flight 93 passengers who revolted against the terrorists on September 11, 2001. In an earlier speech, he also brought the Golden Rule into the equation, explaining that if one wants to fight evil, one should love his neighbor just like he would like to be loved himself.[2] I'm encouraged by these remarks, since similar concepts of citizenship sparked me to such a rewarding career.

Around the time I was in Boy Scouts, my budding thirst for adventure led to an accident in the bathroom that would change my life. This accident thankfully ended my short career in bathtub roller derby. For those who don't know, playing roller derby in the bathtub consists of rubbing soap along the walls of the tub, making it as slick as a luge track, then bravely jumping in and sliding around as long as possible. Once day I slipped and fell on the runner for the sliding glass door, giving myself a five-inch laceration. When I went to our family's doctor, the quality of his care made an impression on me, particularly his skill, attentiveness, and tenderness. Soon afterwards I decided that going into medicine would be the path whereby I could best make my contribution to society, and I made it my career goal.

I moved from Syosset on Long Island, New York, to Cincinnati, Ohio, at the end of junior high school and there met and began dating Linda Stevenson. I attended Wyoming High School and regularly attended Catholic church and my weekly catechism. My faith was important, but I did not have a personal, intimate relationship with God.

Linda and I decided to go to different colleges after high school. I attended Ohio State University for my pre-medical training, and I admit that my faith was very inactive throughout my undergraduate, graduate, and post-graduate training. My motto was "Study hard and play hard." I laid anchor in the library stacks for many hours during the weekdays, mastering the prerequisites for entry into medical school. On the weekends I relieved this pent-up energy with abandon. In retrospect, I thank God I survived the wild parties and revelry.

At the end of my junior year in college, my future in-laws invited me to Linda's older sister's wedding, which I was surprised to be invited to. At this time we renewed our love for each other, and were engaged to be married three months later. We married one week before I started medical school, packed our possessions in a VW Bug, and headed to Houston, where I would attend Baylor College of Medicine.

At Baylor I received an excellent education and developed great confidence in my medical skills and my ability to develop a rapport with patients. I had many caring mentors, including Dr. H. I. Schweppe, Dr. Robert Hall, Dr. Robert Luchi, Dr. David Y. Graham, and Dr. Montague Lane. The motto at Baylor was "See one, do one, teach one," and it instilled the confidence in me not only to treat patients but to instruct and inspire other medical students. I worked extremely hard, and upon graduation I received several honors. I positively glowed with self-assurance.

I then started my internship and residency at Baylor. Interns are often considered the physicians who know the least but do the most. They write all the orders and progress notes that further develop their confidence. A common attitude among these physicians is that they "may not be right, but they are never in doubt."

A jarring encounter with a patient brought me down from my pedestal. One day while making rounds on a fifty-five-year-old man at the Ben Taub General Hospital, the patient informed me that he was going to die that day. I reassured him that his vital signs were stable, his lab tests were all in order, and that in fact I was considering discharging him from the hospital that day. That afternoon the patient had a sudden and unexpected cardiac arrest and died.

I was shaken. We performed a post-mortem examination on the patient and determined that he had developed a sudden, unexpected retroperitoneal bleed (bleeding in the back of the abdomen) and had died from shock. His awareness of his impending death raised new questions in my mind: How did he know he was going to die? To what extent do I control the power over life and death? Who's in charge? Was God trying to tell me something? These early signs of my undeveloped worldview would lead to more intense questioning later on. When I reflect back now on my post-graduate experience, I realize that many of my most critical lessons came from my patients, including one of the answers to the above question, which is that God *is* in control. Accepting that truth helps me keep a rein on the arrogance that doctors are so vulnerable to. A good physician should be both confident in his abilities and humble about his limitations. As 1 Corinthians 1:31 says, "Let him who boasts boast in the Lord."

Patients have also taught me that I shouldn't automatically discard my emotions when I see them. There are conflicting opinions regarding the degree to which physicians should allow emotional attachments to their patients. Dr. William Osler, widely known as one of the fathers of modern internal medicine, favored equanimity,[3] which means "even-mindedness" and "the ability to keep emotions from influencing decisions." When I think of equanimity, I imagine a sea captain guiding his shipmates through an unexpected storm, addressing new problems with a cool quick mind, unfazed by fears for the lives of his mates. The idea of equanimity has a long, honored tradition in medicine—for good reason.

But newer approaches assert that being emotionally involved with patients' lives doesn't necessarily have to be detrimental to the healing process or decision-making. After all, physicians are as human as anyone else, and they often struggle when their patients do poorly, especially when they die. Dr. Bernie Siegel, a pediatric oncology surgeon and well-known author of books about healing, champions an approach called "rational concern." This approach "allows the expression of feelings without impairing the ability to make decisions."[4] In my experience, the resulting intimacy that is established yields profound benefits for the patient and the caregiver. In some ways, the patient can often heal the physician. While I respect the discipline of equanimity, I believe rational concern is a fine complementary discipline.

At the time of the incident at Ben Taub General Hospital, I hadn't yet developed these insights about God's control over a patient's life and the benefits of rational concern.

Following my internal medicine training at Baylor, I

entered the air force and was stationed in Fairborn, Ohio, as a cardiologist for two years. I continued to develop feelings of confidence in my skill as a physician. Linda and I, along with our two young children, Chris and Laurie, moved to Denver, Colorado, in July 1979 to complete my cardiology training at the University of Colorado Health Sciences Center.

As I said, throughout college, medical school, and my post-graduate training, the faith of my wife and me was inactive at best. One day my father-in-law asked my wife why we didn't attend church, and she replied that she had me and that she didn't need church. Basically, she believed we already had everything that we needed. Similarly, I was glowing with accolades, mindful of little outside my family's concerns, and I was tempted by the idea that I had all the answers. However, my wife and I soon realized that something was missing from our lives. This realization became more obvious when the philosophical inquiries of our three-year-old son left us scratching our heads. One day Chris asked us, "Who is God?" and "What is hell?" among other questions we weren't quite prepared for; our most energetic discussions with him up to that point were usually about how many cookies he deserved after dinner. Linda and I looked at each other and realized we didn't have a clue.

We discussed this and felt that we should go back to church to try to find these answers. We started attending Faith Presbyterian Church in Aurora, Colorado, and heard the good news of Christ for the first time as adults and as a married couple. Independently we accepted Jesus Christ as our personal Lord and Savior and began the process of repentance, which means "seeking to change sinful behavior." I felt like I was born again. I felt like Christ was now walking alongside me, and I began trying to model my life after Him.

At that time, like many young couples, we were having some marital issues. Linda began seeing a therapist, who offered free marital counseling at the church. She suggested that Linda get involved in the Navigators 2:7 Bible Study, whose mission statement came from Colossians 2:6–7. It reads:

> So then, just as you received Christ Jesus as Lord, continue to live in him, rooted and built up in him, strengthened in the faith as you were taught, and overflowing with thankfulness.

My wife quickly became close friends with several of the women in the group, but still didn't have a strong faith. At that time she was also troubled by the news that her sister's new baby had been born with a serious heart defect; in fact, the baby's skin had been blue upon delivery. Then one day she experienced what she believed was the physical presence of God. As she recalls:

> I remember one day sitting in bed alone and I just started feeling very despondent and very sad, really sorry that we had moved to Denver. I was also thinking about my sister and her baby and wondering "What if she lost the baby?" My sister was very fragile at that time. I remember sitting in my bed with my knees pulled up to my chest and my hands folded. I started to pray, and as I was praying I felt strong, calloused hands come around mine. I actually felt a physical presence as if these were the Carpenter's hands on mine. It was at that time that I decided to give my life to the Lord and be the person He wanted me to be. I felt that He would be able to give me a new direction and help me to use my gifts to glorify Him and appreciate my life as it was. I was

determined to make my marriage work, and to be a great mom. I believed the Lord had put me in touch with the Navigators 2:7 group because He wanted me to fellowship with these women and remain in His Word.[5]

Some days after this encounter, several of her friends in the study group asked Linda and me to join their Bible fellowship group called the John 2 Koinonia group. *Koinonia* is a Greek word meaning "fellowship." The group consisted of 11 couples who got together every other Sunday evening for an hour of fellowship, an hour of Bible study, and an hour of sharing and personal prayer needs. Today our active involvement and growing relationship with this group and our personal commitments to Christ continue to transform us. It is the fellowship and love of this group that keeps us grounded in Him.

Since coming to know Christ together, my wife and I have experienced a new level of closeness with one another. Linda's love helped me specifically through an episode of depression I suffered during the mid-1990s. It started with the diagnosis of bipolar disorder in our son. I wrongly held myself responsible for his illness, because it is well known that this is a genetic disorder, and my father and his family had suffered from bipolar illness also. For the first time in my life I was dealing with a problem that I couldn't just shake off, and I was not able to "pull myself together," as that popular prescription for depression goes. Looking back on my prayer journals from that time, I notice that my prayer life was as active as ever. I was earnestly seeking God but didn't feel that I had much direction. Luckily, the constant support and encouragement from my wife helped me seek counseling, accept the therapeutic value of medicine, ease my anger, and restore my thinking and peace of mind.

During my depression I felt broken, but I believe God often uses such painful moments to bring people closer to Him and reveal His plans for them. Such moments can be a "special kind of brokenness," as my friend Chuck King describes them. I realized, as Jeremiah 29:11–13 affirms, that God still had a plan for me, plans to prosper me and not to harm me, a plan to give me a hope and a future. He wanted me to seek Him and pray to Him, and I could rest assured that He would listen to me. So I sought Him out with renewed dedication and followed the plans He revealed to me.

I treat my medical practice as a form of ministry. My mission statement is "to care for the physical, emotional, and spiritual needs of my patients." To be a doctor, as Dr. Félix Martí-Ibañez states, "means much more than to dispense pills;" it is "to be an intermediary between man and God."[6]

I must keep God at the forefront of my practice and develop my gifts in accordance with His plan. These gifts include the abilities to listen, communicate, be caring, and leave my patient with a sense of hope. To quote Dr. Martí-Ibañez again, this time on the subject of dealing with patients: "You can cure them sometimes, and you can give them relief often, but hope you can give them always."[7] I firmly agree that when physicians leave the bedside, they should always leave their patient with a sense of hope.

When I think of prayer, I think of a dependent person before the throne of grace, before the throne of God, communicating and asking for guidance and help. This would be an exercise in humility, among other things. As E. M. Bounds wrote in his book, *Power Through Prayer*, "The pride of learning is against the dependent humility of prayer."[8] For someone like me, who once prided himself in knowing all the answers (and who occasionally still falls into that trap), the humbling effects of prayer have been essential to my development as a husband, father, and doctor. This is not meant to belittle the importance of man. According to Bounds, "God's plan is to make much of the man, far more of him than anything else. Men are God's method."[9] Prayer has certainly made me a better man. My hope is that this book renews your prayer life or begins one if you've never had it. I also pray that you will be convinced that God has a plan for you and that this certainty will flood you with hope.

PART 2

PRAYER

CHAPTER 2

PRAYER: DEPENDENT
HUMILITY BEFORE GOD

I strongly suspect that if we saw all the difference even the tiniest
of our prayers make, and all the people those little prayers were
destined to affect, and all the consequences of those prayers down
through the centuries, we would be so paralyzed with awe at the
power of prayer that we would be unable to get up off our knees
for the rest of our lives.

—PETER KREEFT
PROFESSOR OF PHILOSOPHY
BOSTON COLLEGE[1]

Love God. And above all, pray.

—MOTHER TERESA[2]

CHRISTIANS BELIEVE THAT there is a God, that He is a personal God, that He speaks with us, and that He wants to have a relationship with us. Prayer is the means by which people communicate with God; it is an instant, unfailing lifeline to the most important relationship we will ever have.

Carol Osman Brown asserts that "the origins of prayer are lost in antiquity, but there is no known culture that does not use prayer in some form."[3] For Christians, prayer is a fundamental tool in developing our relationship with God.

God is never too busy for our prayers, and He wants to hear from us. One of the most encouraging lessons from Scripture is that when we pray to God with all of our heart, He will always respond to it—maybe not always in the way we want, but always according to His will. As it says in Matthew 7:7, "Ask and it will be given to you; seek and you will find; knock and the door will be opened to you. For everyone who asks receives; he who seeks finds; and to him who knocks, the door will be opened."

In this chapter I will discuss the various types of prayer; examine the roles and uses of prayer in a Christian's life; and share stories about the power of prayer from various pastors, doctors, friends, patients, and the loved ones of patients. I spent many months before the writing of this book interviewing pastors, Christian leaders, and fellow physicians on this subject, many of whom I am blessed to call my friends. To those readers who sometimes pray and feel no connection to God, who have never felt a connection with God, or who don't always like the results of their prayers, I want to assure you that these pastors have struggled with similar problems.

There are many different types of prayer: intercessory, thanksgiving, petitionary, confessional, penitential, corporate, praise, meditative, and prayer in the spirit, among others. Intercessory prayer is praying on someone else's behalf. When offering a prayer of thanksgiving, believers thank God for the numerous blessings they have received. Regarding this type of prayer in the Bible, it says in 1 Thessalonians 5:16–18, "Be joyful always; pray continually; give thanks in all circumstances." A petition is a request or an appeal to God to take care of the needs of one's heart. Second Thessalonians 1:11 addresses petitionary prayer: "With this in mind, we constantly pray for you, that our God may count you worthy of his calling, and that by his power he may fulfill every good purpose of yours." During a confessional prayer, believers admit to God those instances in which they have fallen short of His will. Corporate prayer is a group prayer in which one person speaks aloud or many people take turns speaking, the group ideally united in their sincerity. A prayer of praise acknowledges God for His grace, His mercy, His supremacy, or any of His splendors; it is a way to honor God. A similar type of prayer, the meditative prayer, is a means of contemplating God's characteristics as a reminder of His majesty and grace.

I will spend more time discussing prayer in the spirit, since its legitimacy has historically aroused controversy and its form strikes many as bizarre. Praying in the spirit occurs when the Holy Spirit of God fills someone up and allows him or her to speak in a language the individual has not learned. Praying in the spirit may involve this, but it also goes beyond that. The resulting language can take two forms: it can be a language understood by other men who recognize that tongue, or it can be unintelligible to other people but nevertheless understood by God. The ability to pray in the spirit is a "desirable gift even though it isn't a requirement of faith."[4] Acts 2:4–11 recounts an event called Pentecost when the apostles of Jesus prayed in the Spirit in unison, speaking in languages that they were not familiar with, though their words' meaning was clear to an audience consisting of people who spoke many languages.

I have witnessed others speaking in tongues (praying in the spirit) on several occasions, including the Reverend Setan Lee. Once during a conference for pastors in Cambodia, Reverend Lee was addressing an audience made up predominately of Cambodians. He was translating from English into the Khmer language. While the conference was in progress, a German man came to Pastor Lee and asked if he could share his short testimony to the four hundred pastors and leaders who were present. Pastor Lee then agreed with him and was willing to be his translator. First, the German man shared his testimony in English. About halfway through his speech, the man began to speak German. Pastor Lee continued to translate for the man for about another thirty minutes, although he did not understand or speak any German. After the German man finished his testimony, several German-speaking leaders who were sitting in the audience came up to Pastor Lee and asked, "How long have you been able to speak German?" These men went on to say that Setan's translation of the German man's testimony was perfect.[5]

In New Testament times, the apostle Paul urged people endowed with this gift to interpret the strange language they spoke so that its meaning might benefit others, since otherwise it primarily benefited only the speaker.

Several times I have quoted scripture that encourages people to pray constantly. But what does that mean? Certainly if we spend the whole day kneeling by our beds, hands folded, we would never leave the house. Bud Sparling, a minister at Parker Evangelical Presbyterian Church and former moderator of the General Assembly of the Evangelical Presbyterian Church, asserts that prayer does not require us to speak words or send telepathic messages while being stationary. He said to me:

> Well, prayer is like breathing. It says in the New Testament that we're supposed to pray without ceasing. Some people view that as speaking or directing our thoughts to Him. But I think that prayer for Christians is an attitudinal posture that we live in. I awaken sometimes in the morning conscious that

I'm praying. I'm praying for other people, praying about the day, praying for whatever…it's just a part of my life. I don't think it's something that needs to be clearly initiated all the time. There are specific prayers that people make, like praying in public, or asking someone in the hospital if you can pray with them. In that case you're using speaking aloud. But prayer is not simply words; it's also our connection with God. It is an attitude or a posture. It's an attitude of thankfulness, of openness, of being connected.[6]

Other pastors I spoke with confirmed that prayer can be an attitude and is not limited to spoken words or telepathic messages. Mother Teresa, in her book *Everything Starts with Prayer*, acknowledges that she prays on the move. She says:

You can pray while you work. Small liftings of the mind like, "I love you, God. I trust you, I believe in you, I need you now." Those are wonderful prayers.[7]

Prayer can be as natural and comfortable as having a conversation with a trusted friend. There are no forms that must be followed. There are no complicated verses that must be memorized. *Amen* need not be the concluding word. When the only thoughts a panicking soldier can direct to God are, "Save me, Lord; save me," or if the only request a cancer victim in extreme pain submits to God is, "Help me!" those requests are no less valid prayers than a two-hour, elaborate prayer that a learned pastor might offer on an energetic morning. Dr. Don Sweeting, who has a doctorate in church history and serves as the senior pastor at Cherry Creek Presbyterian Church in Englewood, Colorado, shared some of his ideas on prayer with us.

Prayer is first and foremost an exercise in trust and dependence upon God. Saying that, "We do need you. Life is hard." Secondly, prayer is a communion with God, where we abide with Him, we're in a relationship with Him, and we can enjoy His presence.[8]

Just like a communion with a trusted friend, God invites us to confide in Him. People often feel guilty for sharing too much or demanding too much from their friends, but God wants us to share everything with Him. When we do, we demonstrate our trust and dependence on Him, which is essential to deepening our relationship with Him. When we are frustrated about the decisions we have made, we should recall whether or not we have made our needs known to God. As it says in James 1:5, "If any of you lacks wisdom, he should ask God, who gives generously to all without finding fault, and it will be given to him."

Jesus spoke of the importance of secret, solitary communion with God, as opposed to showy, public prayer, where people often pray in order to demonstrate their supposed holiness to others. In His Sermon on the Mount, recorded in Matthew 6:5–6, He says:

> And when you pray, do not be like the hypocrites, for they love to pray standing in the synagogues and on the street corners to be seen by men. I tell you the truth, they have received their reward in full. But when you pray, go into your room, close the door and pray to your Father, who is unseen. Then your Father, who sees what is done in secret, will reward you.

This passage asserts that there is no better way to improve one's relationship with God than to seek Him out in the privacy of one's heart. God is less interested in how loudly we sing hymns or how frequently we attend church than in the sincerity with which we seek Him through prayer. Dr. Jim Dixon, the senior pastor at Cherry Hills Community Church in Highlands Ranch, Colorado, refers to this type of prayer as "closet prayer," which he considers "pure joy."[9] E. M. Bounds, when discussing the heroism of the first Christians, wrote that those men and women's "profoundest convictions were born in his secret communion with God."[10] God is an ever-present source of wisdom that can be accessed without ceremony, in the privacy of a quiet room or in the midst of a crowded subway car. He is not only willing but eager to listen to us. In prayerful communion we find strength in His presence and direction for our lives.

On His Sermon on the Mount, Jesus offered the Lord's Prayer to His disciples, which can be viewed as a blueprint for how Christians can pray. It contains many of the types of prayers that we mentioned earlier.

> This, then, is how you should pray: "Our Father in heaven, hallowed be your name, your kingdom come, your will be done on earth as it is in heaven. Give us today our daily bread. Forgive us our debts, as we also have forgiven our debtors. And lead us not into temptation, but deliver us from the evil one."
> —MATTHEW 6:9–13

This prayer is justifiably well known; it contains many of the priorities required for a well-developed communion with God. In this prayer the believer acknowledges God's supremacy, pledges support for the realization of God's master plan on Earth and in heaven, admits his humility before and dependence upon God, acknowledges his shortcomings and need for forgiveness, and requests the strength to resist the corrupting power of Satan.

Matthew 6:9, "Our Father in heaven, hallowed be your name," acknowledges that the person praying is entering God's presence and affirming His holiness. There are many names for God that emphasize different aspects of His divinity. One of these names, as Dr. Bob Beltz explains in his book, *Transforming Your Prayer Life*, can be translated as *Yahweh-rophe*, which emphasizes that "healing is intimately linked to God's very Nature." According to Dr. Beltz, in Exodus 15:26, God promised His people that "if they lived in obedience (which they failed to do), He would keep them from being afflicted with the diseases of Egypt. Then he spoke His name: YHWH-rophe, 'I am the Lord who heals you.'"[11]

I sometimes direct my own prayers to the name of Yahweh-rophe, especially on behalf of my patients, since this aspect of God's nature is so central in the context of patient care.

The verse of the Lord's Prayer, "Your kingdom come, your will be done" (Matt. 6:10), expresses an obedience to God's will on Earth and in the afterlife. "Give us today our daily bread" (v. 11), affirms that God is our sustainer and our provider and is a petition for Him to take care of our needs according to His will. "Forgive us our debts, as we also have forgiven our debtors" (v. 12), is partly a prayer of confession in which we admit that we are sinners and that only God has the power to completely forgive us. It also expresses obedience to Jesus' command to forgive our enemies, with an implicit understanding that if we cannot do that we cannot expect to be forgiven ourselves. As this book will later discuss in more detail, especially in the stories of Reverend Lee and a woman I will call Diane, forgiveness is essential in transforming us into the man or woman God wants us to be. In the context of dying patients, words of forgiveness can be more essential to healing and peace of mind than the most expensive treatments. Along with prayer, it is fundamental to the way Yahweh-rophe works. "Praise the LORD," begins Psalm 103, "who forgives all your sins and heals all your diseases" (v. 3).

The verse, "And lead us not into temptation but deliver us from the evil one" (Matt. 6:13), is a petition to God to grant us the ability to recognize temptations in our life. Once we recognize them, we request that God give us the strength and wisdom to overcome the temptations of Satan and choose God's way instead.

Dr. Sweeting pointed out that the Lord's Prayer is "a springboard believers can use to get you started, but you don't have to be confined to it."[12] It contains many different forms of prayer (praise, petition, confessional, etc.) and stresses core attributes of our relationship with God; therefore, it acts as the foundation from which we can submit more personal, specific prayers.

Becoming a faithful prayer warrior is not easy; the benefits of prayer are not always obvious. Who, in the midst of a prayer attempt on their knees with hands folded, hasn't occasionally felt a little silly and even remote from any feeling of connection to a higher power? And everyone knows that even when hundreds of people band together and pray for the life of a dying patient, those requests are not always granted in the ways people want. Without warning, loved ones die before we have a chance to say good-bye, and our prayers sometimes seem to be in vain. For many, enough discouraging experiences with prayer make them abandon it forever. Faith can be the best remedy to this struggle, as our ability to communicate with God depends in large measure on our faith. Hebrews 11:6 reads:

> And without faith it is impossible to please God, because anyone who comes to him must believe that he exists and that he rewards those who earnestly seek him.

Pastor Bud Sparling adds:

> I don't see how you can separate prayer from faith. What good is prayer if you don't believe you're talking to someone? There's not going to be a result. Sometimes, of course, there are people without much of a belief in God, who are driven to prayer by a crisis. It's too bad that so many people see prayer as the last resource instead of the first. Paul says in Thessalonians [5:17–18] to pray in all circumstances.[13]

This crisis can be the foxhole of war or the illness of a dying patient. I've been blessed to witness numerous patients develop a prayer life for the first time at the end of their lives. In these situations, faith was present at the same time. But the more removed we are from such crises, the less we feel dependent on God.

Faith can fluctuate even among the leaders of the church, let alone for people for whom God is less central in their lives. For those of you who struggle with your prayer life or who have never had a sustained prayer life, take heart at the admissions of Dr. Sweeting:

> There are times when I can't pray; there are many reasons for that, sometimes I just don't feel Him. Maybe I'm having a bad day, I'm feeling disappointment, or my connection just seems cold; there are seasons like that.[14]

In addition to simply not feeling God's presence at times, Dr. Sweeting believes his own human nature sometimes keeps him from successful prayer:

> There's something in my nature that fights against prayer and resists it. It's the aspect of my nature that rebels against God, [the part of my nature] which feels self-sufficient. Dependence does not come easy; I like to do things my way. That's the biggest battle of my prayer life. It divides my nature. It makes me want to shut him out.[15]

Prayer, after all, as a previous quotation of Dr. Sweeting's insisted, should be an exercise in dependence, or better yet, as the E. M. Bounds quote asserted in the previous chapter, an exercise in "dependent humility." So these attitudes of dependent humility, coupled with faith, are two crucial ingredients in developing or sustaining a meaningful prayer life.

This dependent humility is also essential when we are interceding on someone else's behalf. Because this issue relates to the dynamic between doctor and patient, I will give a short summary of my experiences speaking on this subject.

I have been called to speak on prayer and medicine since 1993. I've given talks on the subject at churches, medical conferences, medical schools, and nursing conferences. I've been interviewed by the *Denver Post*, local television news programs, and local radio programs. Dr. Tom Newman and Dr. Linda Williams joined me for prayer and medicine symposiums starting in 2005. Their insights and experiences will be included into this and other chapters, so I will introduce them briefly.

Dr. Linda Williams worked as a family practice physician for over 10 years. She's also received some training in psychiatry with Dr. Karl Menninger, a notable figure in his field. In addition to teaching at Denver Seminary, she has done extensive overseas mission work in Kenya, Argentina, Peru, Taiwan, Hong Kong, Thailand, China, and most recently with a team I led to Cambodia in January of 2008. In July 2008, she started a psychiatry residency program a the Harvard Medical School to complete her psychiatry training.

Dr. Williams's faith is central to the guiding principles behind her solo practice, as she shared with me: "When I started, I was the first full-time family practice physician who was a female. The male doctors didn't really know what to make of me. Since I didn't have a tangible partner, I prayed from day one that Jesus would be my partner and give me wisdom and discernment and compassion for my patients."[16]

Dr. Thomas Newman is a Denver internist who is also a member the Association of Christian Therapists (ACT). Both Dr. Newman and Dr. Williams share my interest in the use of personal prayer in the context of patient care.

Dr. Newman attended the ACT Conference in the spring of 1981, and he heard Sister Briege McKenna share her insight into prayer and healing. Sister McKenna is a Catholic nun from Ireland who had been ministering to the sick through intercessory prayer. Many of her patients have suffered from cancer. Here is Dr. Newman's account of what the sister told us:

> She was coming back from a communion service when she had this inner vision of everyone being a sort of a "battered tent." The fact she too was a battered tent had to do with her own brokenness. In the vision Jesus approached her tent and was starting to come in, but she didn't want to let Him in.
>
> In response Jesus said, "I live here," at which point she *did* let him in. Jesus said, "You know, Briege,

your problem is that you try to do everything your-self. But when people are coming to you, they are really coming to *Me*. So if you'll just step aside, I will meet their need."[17]

Dr. Newman said he has examined the meaning of that vision many times. He said:

It reminds me not to get in the way of whatever Jesus is trying to do. When I am praying with patients, or I'm praying with others, it is uncommon for me to pray out loud—unless there's a specific reason to—because praying out loud is so often a distraction. If somebody prays out loud around me, I end up listening. Partly the distraction comes from people's reaction to prayers that are sermons, or what I call sermon-prayers, which are so common. Many people don't like sermon-prayers, and it makes them break off their own connection with God. So I've found that when I'm praying silently, there's no problem.

When I pray, sometimes I tell patients what I'd like them to focus on. I say, "Just picture Jesus. Tell him your problems; tell Him how you feel." I use the word "feel" because I want it to be from the heart. That way, in the silence of their hearts, with privacy from the outside world, they can honestly tell Him whatever they want. Meanwhile I'm praying silently too. I may be asking specifically for what they want, but I'm also asking for guidance. I'm also praying, "Jesus, let them palpably feel your presence, your love, and your peace."

So it's all silent. And what's remarkable is that He does a better job of letting them know who He is than what I could say. He simply enters into it

His way for that person. I have no question that He responds to every prayer in His way.[18]

I agree we need to get out of Jesus' way and let Him do the healing. But doctors are often pressured to avoid bringing up the subject of prayer. Some people in administrative medicine set rules against praying audibly with patients—even when patients give explicit permission. Some of them even make rules about broaching the subject. Even when explicit rules aren't set, such activities are often frowned upon as violating patient boundaries and risking lawsuits. However, when patients are known to have a faith and ask to be prayed for, shouldn't doctors who share this faith be allowed to participate in an activity that they believe yields such benefits, provides such hope, and increases doctor–patient intimacy?

As Dr. Newman says, "There are God's rules and there are man's rules. Sometimes those rules conflict. God would have you pray. It can always be done silently."[19] I agree with Dr. Newman. I will follow the Lord's directions. If a physician is sensitive enough, he can usually determine when patients are comfortable and eager to be prayed for or with. In more delicate situations, prayer can be done silently.

Dr. Newman's insights on silent prayer echo those of Pastor Bud Sparling. As Dr. Newman says. "In every aspect of our lives, as we go through our day, we can be calling on Him, saying, 'Thank You, Lord,' and moving on. Sometimes it bubbles up and is a more active form of prayer. Other times it settles down, but it's continual."[20] Dr. Newman goes to on to make a crucial point too often ignored: "Prayer is not just powerful in itself. Prayer is powerful because of who it is connected to; it is connected to God."[21]

Are mere hopeful thoughts directed at the sky powerful?

When we mentally reach out for help indiscriminately to any force beyond ourselves, "accepting all takers," so to speak, is that powerful? I don't think so. I don't have faith in the power of any prayer that isn't centered on God.

Dr. Newman continues by saying that when people come to a physician, a therapist, a nurse, etc., they come to a healer. In our society, our degrees, training, scientific skills, and stethoscopes are outward signs of being a healer. We listen, examine, diagnose, and then treat to the limits of our skills and science. We acknowledge these limits. I approach praying with a patient by asking the patient if he or she would like to pray a prayer together in silence. I pray silently to get out of Jesus' way. I tell the patient that Jesus understands, that in His heart He has experienced what he or she is feeling or going through. I ask the person to picture Jesus and tell Him what is on his heart, how he feels, what he requests of Him—whatever comes to mind. I intercede while the patient is doing this, pleading with Jesus to pour out His love on that person and respond to his or her need, all in silence. I usually rest my hand on a hand or shoulder and rarely, but occasionally, on the person's head. As caring physicians, nurses, or therapists, we need to recognize our limits and step aside to allow the Master Healer to do His work.

How can we resolve the issue that our prayers are not always answered in the ways we want? After all, as mentioned before, Jesus said, "For everyone who asks receives; he who seeks finds; and to him who knocks, the door will be opened" (Matt. 7:8). Dr. Dixon warns people not to interpret this statement as meaning that we should expect God to answer our prayers as if *our* expectations were the measurement of success. He believes we should keep in mind that it is God's will we are invoking; we should not view prayer as a means to receive an automatic handout of all our desires. If we pray for a new Lexus but continue to sputter along in our old Chevy, we should consider whether or not our will is aligned with God's before we question the legitimacy of prayer. Dr. Dixon uses the term *name-it-and-claim-it prayers* to refer to prayers in which people demand quick, concrete responses to their desires. He says:

> There's a whole segment of the Christian world that believes in "name-it-and-claim-it" prayers. They think that if we can just garner enough faith or say the right words or keep ourselves pure enough, God will always heal us. Some people believe that if He doesn't heal us then there's something wrong with us in terms of our morality. I do believe that God heals, but He's sovereign and there's a great mystery to how His healing is delivered. When I'm praying for someone to be healed, my understanding of the Scriptures is that we should pray for the desires of our heart. But there's hopefully submissiveness when we pray that reflects not our will but His.[22]

Dr. Sweeting elaborates on this "great mystery" by using the example of a prayer made so that a sick person will get better. He insists that the deepening of one's relationship with God is the most important outcome of such a prayer. He says:

> That relationship with God is the ultimate issue. The ultimate issue is not us getting better. That's idolatry. God's healing is not always done in this life. Often people pray for healing in this life. The ultimate healing is when we die and we go into the presence of the Lord and we get the resurrection body. Often we pray for short-term stuff. Sometimes I tell people that

God may heal you by bringing you into His presence.
I don't know if a nonbeliever will believe that.[23]

These comments, like Dr. Dixon's, remind us that when praying we should keep in mind that God will answer our prayers according to His plan for us, not our own, and that doubting Him on the basis of unsatisfactory responses to our prayers is presumptuous; it is like claiming to know God's master plan. After all, we have all fallen from grace, and the desires of our heart, if granted without exception, would only corrupt us. In such a scenario, our favorite football team might never lose, we might be wealthy enough to retire by forty, or we might have dominion over the earth, but such happenings would have little to do with God's plan for us.

What else determines the potency of our prayers? Are the prayers of a priest automatically more powerful than those of a prostitute? Can the opposite be true? In James 5:16, the Bible says, "The prayer of a righteous man is powerful and effective." Dr. Sweeting suggests that in the case of church elders laying hands on someone and praying for them, the righteousness of each of the elders can influence the power of the prayers. When he uses the word *you* below, he is referring to such elders.

> You need to be clean. You need to have your sins confessed if you're going to put yourself in this position. If you're going to be an instrument of God, to bring comfort and healing to people, then you are a channel. I don't understand this exactly; but somehow His work is in you and if you are unclean it gums up the works. There are a lot of prayer-busters, and that's one of them. You have to do business with God before you do this.[24]

Which aspects of a man's righteousness contribute to the potency of his prayers? What about the daily prayers of people who aren't church leaders? As we've already discussed, successful prayer is hard to imagine without some measure of faith. And petitioning God with arrogance or anger is not an attitude that is likely to establish the sort of connection that dependent humility creates. According to the Bible, our treatment of neighbors also affects the success of our prayers. In 1 Peter 3:7, the Bible warns men to be considerate toward their wives and treat them with respect, "so that nothing will hinder your prayers." Sincerity seems to be another factor in the effectiveness of prayers. Recall the quote from Jeremiah in which God promises that "you will seek me and find me when you seek me with all your heart" (Jer. 29:13). Later, in Hebrews 10:22, the Bible urges men to "draw near God with a sincere heart in full assurance of faith." If we choose instead to pray only so that others will hear us, and God truly knows our innermost feelings, He will certainly tell the difference.

You may wonder if I believe God only heeds the prayers of Christians, since my own perspective is so heavily influenced by my Christian faith. I do not believe so; neither do any of the pastors I spoke with. Dr. Jim Dixon reminded us that some time ago a former head of the Baptist Convention made a highly publicized statement that God doesn't hear the prayer of a Jew. Dr. Dixon says:

> That's a ludicrous statement. God hears whatever prayer he wants to; He loves people all over the world. My guess is God hears all prayers, and can certainly respond to whatever He wants to. I don't think all Christian prayer is equal. The Bible says the prayer of a righteous man has a great power. *Righteous:*

that word in that passage means a right relationship to God. It's a quality of holiness; it's the mark of
someone who's living in submission to God's will. I
believe Jesus is present in other cultures.[25]

We as Christians must be careful not to judge other Christians and non-Christians regarding the character of their
heart. God alone can make such judgments. C. S. Lewis, in
his famous book *Mere Christianity*, also discusses the difficulty of judging non-Christians.

> There are people (a great many of them) who are
> slowly ceasing to be Christians but who still call
> themselves by that name: some of them are cler-
> gymen. There are other people who are slowly
> becoming Christians though they do not yet call
> themselves so. There are people who do not accept
> the full Christian doctrine about Christ but who
> are so strongly attracted by Him that they are His
> in a much deeper sense than they themselves under-
> stand. There are people in other religions who are
> being led by God's secret influence (amazing grace)
> to concentrate on those parts of their religion which
> are in agreement with Christianity, and who thus
> belong to Christ without knowing it. For example, a
> Buddhist of good will may be led to concentrate more
> and more on the Buddhist teaching about mercy and
> to leave in the background (though he might still
> say he believed) the Buddhist teaching on certain
> other points. Many of the good Pagans long before
> Christ's birth may have been in this position. And
> always, of course, there are a great many people who
> are just confused in mind and have a lot of incon-
> sistent beliefs all jumbled up together. Consequently,

it is not much use trying to make judgments about Christians and non-Christians in the mass.[26]

So a man of any religious background whose attitude is one of submission towards God and who values the Commandments, even if he's never heard the commandments, can be pleasing in God's eye and have his prayers answered. Dr. Sweeting points out an episode in Acts 10 in which a Roman centurion had his prayers answered by God. Dr. Sweeting says:

> There are some who say God doesn't hear the prayer of an unbeliever. I think that's an inadequate answer. God hears the prayer of everyone because he's All-knowing. There's the example of Cornelius from the New Testament. He's within the Jewish camp but he's not fully Orthodox. He discovers Jesus through Peter. He's a God-fearing man, and the Bible tells us that God hears his prayers. Also, there are examples in the Bible where God doesn't listen to the prayers of believers. The Bible says God will not listen to your prayers if you harbor iniquity in your heart.[27]

It is a mystery to me how God is able to send the right person or information to the millions of people who have not come to know God, let alone be exposed to the good news of Christ. But I can believe that God acknowledges those who seek truth and a relationship with Him with all their strength. The comments by these pastors and physicians and by the Bible reinforce what I've discussed about how crucial our attitudes are in approaching and connecting with God. What's fundamental is that we pray in a spirit of dependent humility, sincere in our desire to know God better. We should not be shy about sharing our innermost thoughts and requests, but we should be careful that we pray that His will would be done and not ours. Our relationship with God is the ultimate issue.

PART 3

PATIENT STORIES

CHAPTER 3

KASEY'S STORY: NEAR-DEATH VISION of the CITY of GOD

M Y INTERACTIONS WITH Kasey, whose story I previewed in chapter 1, fortified my conviction that prayer has powerful consequences and that the afterlife and the City of God, as described in the Book of Revelation, are realities.

After cardiac and respiratory failure, Kasey wavered for three days between life and death. During her out-of-body experience, when she was physically unconscious, she had a vision that she later described as much more vivid than just a dream. In this vision, she witnessed images straight out of the Bible that she had never read about, she came into the presence of God, and she observed events and conversations that took place within miles of her hospital room that she was later able to describe with perfect accuracy. She also heard the distinct voices of several people who prayed for her during those three days, both audibly and silently, and later found that her account of what they had prayed matched up word for word. She ended up stabilizing, against my predictions, and though she died five years later as a result of her health problems, she spent her last years conveying the message that God hears the prayers of the faithful. She spread this message with such memorable conviction and warmth that she left a lasting impression with those blessed enough to have known her.

I first encountered Kasey on December 30, 1988, at around 4:45 p.m. That afternoon, as I mentioned, I had 15 minutes before I could turn new patients over to my partner, who was on call. The next day I was planning on leaving on a Caribbean cruise with my family. Suddenly I was called in to see this young, married, 35-year-old AT&T worker who was in shock.

I drove from my office to Swedish Medical Center and found that Kasey's skin was blue, she had a heart rate of 180, and her systolic blood pressure was only 60 mm Hg (normal pressure is over 90 mm Hg). She had been admitted with a history of respiratory failure, and while in the hospital she had a respiratory arrest, which required her to have a breathing tube put in. Shortly thereafter she began having serious cardiac arrhythmias (heartbeat irregularities) and a cardiac arrest (due to ventricular tachycardia and ventricular fibrillation). These conditions caused her heart to stop beating, effectively cutting off blood flow from her heart. She received electrical countershocks to restart her heart.

When I arrived I was unclear about the cause of her respiratory failure and cardiac arrest. I was barking commands and ordering emergency tests, including an echocardiogram, which uses sound waves to image the heart and its function. The test showed that her heart wasn't contracting well. I inserted a Swan-Ganz catheter into her neck vein and passed this catheter into the lung to measure the pressure in the lung so that I might better determine which medicines to give her and which actions to take. This step helped us determine that her cardiac function was not compatible with life. The catheter revealed that she had a cardiac output of one liter per minute (normal is five liters per minute) and a pulmonary capillary wedge pressure of 40 (normal is less than 20). I started her on several special medications. I put a special balloon catheter (intra-aortic balloon) into her right femoral artery to increase her blood pressure and blood flow, and hopefully save her life. At this point I wasn't sure if she had sustained a heart attack or if she needed a heart-lung transplant, or both.

After four hours of working on her I had gotten nowhere. Her blood pressure was still very low, and her cardiac output was still not compatible with life. I went into the waiting room and talked to her husband, Jim. I told him that Kasey's prognosis was poor, that I didn't believe she would make it, and I suggested ways he might break the news to their five-year-old son. I went back into the room and brushed the bloody hair off of Kasey's face and prayed in an audible tone: "I've done all I can do. The rest is up to you, Lord." Then I went home and wept. My wife comforted me, and the next day we left for a restful vacation.

When I came back I was fully expecting Kasey to have died. In fact, she was off the breathing machine and out of the intensive care unit. She didn't recognize me, and when I recommended several cardiac studies, she refused them, being the feisty, stubborn, extraordinary patient she was. These tests included a cardiac catheterization. This is an invasive cardiac test where catheters are inserted into the groin artery and advanced to the heart. This test measures coronary blood flow and cardiac function and may have revealed some of the reasons for her cardiac arrest and dysfunction. Since she was doing so much better, I signed off on her case. She was ultimately discharged on February 2.

My next interaction with her occurred when she mailed me a letter containing her testimony. I will now present the story from her perspective, including the testimony she gave at Calvary Temple Church, where she was a member.

KASEY'S TESTIMONY

I will first recount what happened to me in the physical and then describe what happened in the spiritual.

I've spent the last 20 years being treated as a severe asthmatic. With this last hospitalization, my doctor finally discovered that I have a rare genetic disorder called Alpha–1 antitrypsin deficiency. A specific enzyme produced by the body to protect the lining of the lungs is produced in insufficient quantities by my liver and is the root of my problem. My lung capacity was less than half of a normal person's, and my ability to expel air from my lungs was only 25 percent of a normal person's.

December 1988 came about, and I had been wrestled with three bouts of the flu. I convinced myself that I'd take some time off from work and spend the Christmas holidays recuperating. But in my never ending pursuit to be supermom, I continued to work crazy hours and spent the holidays making 96 decorated cutout cookies for my son while I completed the last of the Christmas shopping. I felt so terrible that I barely remember the gift-exchanging that took place on Christmas Day. But the super-mom syndrome rose within me once more as I forced myself into the kitchen to begin preparing the stuffing for the Cornish hens I'd planned for dinner. I managed to get the hens stuffed and into the oven before I collapsed in a chair in the den. Finally I asked my husband, Jim, to pack a bag for me, drive me to the hospital, and be sure to put in my Bible. As we drove to the hospital, Jim prayed for me, asking the Lord to relax my breathing.

From Christmas Day until December 30, I sat in a hospital room with my legs crossed Indian-fashion on the bed and my arms leaning on the bed table to support my upper torso. I couldn't lie down; I couldn't rest; I couldn't sleep or eat. Every ounce of energy was directed to the very difficult effort of breathing.

I requested that I be transferred to intensive care. By December 30, I knew I was deteriorating and that I was going to go into arrest. The medications were no longer working; in fact, they were causing a rebounding effect. When rebounding occurs, the airways in the lungs actually begin to constrict rather that dilate. As a respiratory therapist administered an inhalation treatment, I implored him to call my doctor.

"I'm going into arrest," I told him.

"No. Your blood gases are fine. You'll be OK," he responded.

"Please, call him. I'm going into arrest," I begged.

"Just relax," the therapist said. "Everything will be fine."

"Read my lips," I said, in a not-too-pleasant voice. "I'm going into arrest."

And with those final words, I died.

I went into respiratory arrest. As they labored to get the tubes down my nose and into my lungs to hook me up to the respirator, I went into cardiac arrest. They spent four hours doing CPR on me. It took three electroshocks to get my heart beating again. But my blood pressure was so low they decided to hook me up to a heart pump to ensure a sufficient amount of blood was flowing. For three days I hovered between life and death, kept alive only by life support equipment. The doctors alternately considered either performing a heart–lung transplant, which would necessitate transporting me to another hospital, or simply disconnecting me from the life support equipment. That's where I was in the physical.

In the spiritual, an entirely different experience was occurring. At the point where I died, I journeyed in the spiritual to another "place." I opened my eyes to a beautiful structure. It appeared to be made of stones, yet each layer shone with glorious colors that made me think of precious stones. I saw greens and yellows and blues and reds. The highest level I could see shone like topaz, yet I knew I was not seeing the top of this structure. In trying to describe this stone edifice, I've said it was like a castle, but I knew it wasn't a castle; a temple like the temple in Jerusalem, yet I knew it wasn't a temple. It had gates. I knew somehow that if I went through the gates I'd pass from life to death. I did not approach the gates. The ground surrounding the temple shone with light. In fact, light emanated from everything around me. I remember that the ground shone like transparent glass, but when I looked closely, it wasn't glass.

I found myself enveloped by a resounding chorus of voices and music. If you listen to a choir, you hear the blending of many separate voices into one harmony. Yet, if you listen carefully, you can hear the separate sounds of the altos, sopranos, tenors, and basses. If you listen even more closely, you can hear individual voices. Such was my experience. I realized the voices I heard were the voices of people in prayer. The thought suddenly crossed my mind that the voices I heard were those of people from Calvary Temple [the name of Kasey's church], and it suddenly occurred to me that someone must have called the prayer line. I was very comforted. I then distinguished individual voices from the chorus. I heard first the voice of one of my pastors lifted in prayer. Then I heard the sweet, melodious voice of another pastor and realized he, too, was praying. Next I heard the voice of one of our Bible study members. And then I heard a voice booming over the rest. I did not know whose this was, but I distinctly remember this person saying "and the gates of darkness shall not prevail."

Weeks later, after I was released from intensive care and the life support equipment was disconnected so I could finally talk, I was excitedly retelling these events to my husband. I learned then that [both the pastors whose prayers I heard in the spirit] had come to pray for me in the hospital. When I shared my testimony with [the Bible study member whom I had heard], I discovered he too had come to the hospital. He told me he had prayed silently in the spirit, yet I clearly had heard his voice. While in the hospital, another man came to visit me…When he spoke I realized that the fourth, booming voice belonged to him.

As the chorus of voices continued to grow louder and louder, I became aware of a great celebration feast being prepared. A dove was being prepared, along with what appeared to be a broth made from the dove. I was aware of a presence, which I knew to be the Lord. The Lord then spoke to me and explained that many believed that the dove and the broth held special healing properties. He told me if I ate of the flesh of the dove and drank from the cup that I would be made well. As the elements were offered to me, I did as I was instructed. Suddenly there was a profound silence. All of the voices were quieted. I looked up when I heard the crack and snap of what sounded like a blanket being shaken out in the wind. I saw a blanket of feathers being spread over me and knew the moment it touched me I would be protected so that nothing on Earth could harm me. I knew I was covered by the Holy Spirit.

I heard the Lord's voice speak one more time. He told me that He had heard the prayer of faith and the prayers of the faithful raised for me. The words from James 5:14–16 came to my mind as the Lord spoke:

> Is any one of you sick? He should call the elders of the church to pray over him and anoint him with oil in the name of the Lord. And the prayer offered in faith will make the sick person well; the Lord will raise him up. If he has sinned, he will be forgiven. Therefore confess your sins to each other and pray for each other so that you may be healed. The prayer of a righteous man is powerful and effective.

The Lord then told me that it was not yet my time, that my mission in life had not yet been fulfilled. He told me that the prayer of faith was calling me back and that I must return. I awoke to the voice of one of my doctors repeatedly calling my name.

It has taken me time to sort through what happened to me and to understand the meaning of what I saw and heard. After I returned home, the wife of one of my pastors shared with me...Psalm 91:4, which still runs shivers up and down my spine each time I read it:

> He will cover you with his feathers, and under his wings you will find refuge; his faithfulness will be your shield and rampart.

Shortly afterwards, I received a call from my best high school friend, who is an Episcopal minister. She asked me if I'd seen a tunnel and a light at the end of the tunnel. I told her no. The light I'd seen was different. I tried to explain to her how the light simply shone from everything around me, yet had no apparent source.

Our talk led us to the Book of Revelation. I'm embarrassed to admit that I am probably one of the few Christians who has never read that book. I'd always wanted to believe in the Second Coming but I didn't want to know a whole lot of details about it. However, I found myself turning to Revelation 21, and my eyes fell on verses 18–23:

> The wall was made of jasper, and the city of pure gold, as pure as glass. The foundations of the city walls were decorated with every kind of precious stone. The first foundation was jasper, the second sapphire, the third chalcedony, the fourth emerald, the fifth sardonyx, the

sixth carnelian, the seventh chrysolite, the eighth beryl, the ninth topaz, the tenth chrysoprase, the eleventh jacinth, and the twelfth amethyst. The twelve gates were twelve pearls, each gate made of a single pearl. The great street of the city was of pure gold, like transparent glass. I did not see a temple in the city, because the Lord God Almighty and the Lamb are its temple. The city does not need the sun or the moon to shine on it, for the glory of God gives it light, and the Lamb is its lamp.

I was unfamiliar with many of the words in these verses so I took the time to look them up in the dictionary. I discovered many of them referred to different colored quartz stones as well as semi-precious stones. The colors leaped out at me: reds, greens, blues and yellows—my topaz. I knew that in this passage I'd found the description of the place I had seen. St. John had to have seen it too. It was the same.

I spent six weeks in the hospital and another six weeks recovering at home. Having lost all of my muscles, I had to painfully learn to sit, stand, walk, and feed myself again. I targeted Easter Sunday to be the first day I ventured from the house. We actually made it two Sundays before Easter. We asked our pastor to serve us communion. I felt a compelling need to celebrate in the "feast" one more time.

For all of you who prayed for me as I lay critically ill, I offer my sincere and humble thanks. Be assured your prayers are heard by the Lord. I, too, was blessed by the experience of hearing your voices.

I am convinced that I live today because of your faithfulness in prayer. When you are discouraged, try to remember that the Lord does hear the prayer of faith and the prayers of the faithful.

I will end by sharing this word. Psalm 150 has held special meaning for me since I've suffered so many years with breathing difficulties. Every night I've ended my day by saying, "Let everything that has breath praise the LORD" [Ps. 150:6]. But last year our pastor shared a story with our Corinthian class about his father. Apparently he also suffered with a breathing problem. He told us that each day his father said, "With every breath that thou lendest me I will praise the Lord." I now end each day by saying: "With every breath that thou lendest me, O Lord, I will praise thy name."[1]

After Kasey recovered, she recalled other details from her out-of-body experience that she wanted to share with her doctors. Though she was concerned about how they might perceive her claims, she was convinced that her visions had taken place in real life, and after praying about it she decided to confront her doctors. First she approached Dr. Mountain. She claimed that while she had been unconscious she had seen Dr. Mountain climb into a blue jeep in order to drive to the hospital. Kasey had never seen his car before, nor had she know where he lived. She saw him receive the call about her condition along the way. She recalled that there had been snow on the ground. She recalled the exact route he had taken. Once he arrived at her side, she claimed that she had seen him remove the cross she wore around her neck and that this had upset her. Dr. Mountain, in amazement, confirmed all these details. According to Kasey, he basically accepted what had been going on in the spiritual as the only way that she could have known what was going on in the physical as well. He told her, "I just don't understand how you were aware of everything that was going on. You were clinically dead; at most you were comatose. You should not have known."[2]

When I asked Dr. Mountain about how his interaction with Kasey affected him, he felt that it made him a better listener and a better physician. I found Kasey's testimony to be extremely moving. It validated for me the power of prayer and the accuracy of Scripture.

A week after I received her testimony, she showed up at my office unannounced. That day she had an appointment with Dr. Mountain, whose office was located on the second floor of the office building where I also worked. She knew that my own office was on the fifth floor. She walked in and asked to speak with me without an appointment, which as you might imagine normally requires a long wait, to say the least. Nevertheless, I agreed to meet with her promptly.

The first thing I told her was that I was also a Christian. She told me later this had made it much easier for her to open up to me. That day I was wearing my green surgical scrubs. Seeing me in this outfit, which I had been wearing the day of her clinical death, triggered a series of memories from her out-of-body experience. Once she was home she realized that I also had been in her visions. She had not recalled this when I had met her during her recovery since I had on a dress shirt and bow tie.

In her visions, she remembered me hovering over her wearing my surgical mask. She recalled that I had inserted one catheter into her neck and another catheter into her groin. She had seen me take off my mask, brush the bloody hair from her face, and say, "I've done all I can do. The rest is up to You, Lord." She later said this gesture had struck her as being tender, remembering that she had been bothered about how dirty her hair had been. I confirmed that all these physical details had taken place exactly as she remembered.

In another letter Kasey shared with me a verse that she believed God had directed her to give to me, which has become a special verse to me. It opens chapter 1 of this book—Jeremiah 29:11–13. Kasey also told me that after our meeting she felt that the burden on her heart had been lifted. I responded that I now felt that burden had passed on to me. That burden took the form of a need to share Kasey's story and also my beliefs in the power of prayer in general with other people.

In Kasey's last years she often said how blessed she felt to have been given more life. She compared her experience to that of Hezekiah, a king of Judah who also experienced the power of prayer. In 2 Kings 20:1–6 the Bible reads:

> In those days Hezekiah became ill and was at the point of death. The prophet Isaiah son of Amoz went to him and said, "This is what the LORD says: Put your house in order, because you are going to die; you will not recover." Hezekiah turned his face to the wall and prayed to the LORD, "Remember, O LORD, how I have walked before you faithfully and with wholehearted devotion and have done what is good in your eyes." And Hezekiah wept bitterly. Before Isaiah had left the middle court, the word of the LORD came to him: "Go back and tell Hezekiah, the leader of my people, 'This is what the LORD, the God of your father David, says: I have heard your

prayer and seen your tears; I will heal you. On the third day from now you will go up to the temple of the LORD. I will add fifteen years to your life.'"

Kasey said afterwards that just as Hezekiah's prayer had influenced God, so had the prayers of her friends and loved ones influenced God into giving her more time.

I invited Kasey to share her testimony with the John 2 Koinonia Bible study group to which my wife and I belong. At the time she spoke to us, the group was studying the Book of Revelation. The study seemed particularly significant, considering how similar Kasey's vision of the city corresponded to the account of the risen City of Jerusalem as described in chapter 21 of Revelation. Like many students of Revelation, we were unclear about whether certain sections of the book were intended to be read literally or symbolically. Kasey's testimony convinced many of us that our visions of heaven, which we treasured so deeply, were grounded in reality. Kasey and I later discussed her testimony on a local Christian radio station and also at the Trinity Evangelical Presbyterian Church.

In Kasey's testimony regarding the city, she recalls that "the ground shone like transparent glass, but when I looked closely, it wasn't glass." In Revelation 21 the Bible reads, "The city [was] of pure gold, like unto clear glass" (v. 18). She describes seeing "greens and yellows and blues and reds... and the highest level I could see shone like topaz; yet I knew I wasn't seeing the top of this structure."[3] Among the 12 foundations of the city described in Revelation are jasper, which is an opaque red, yellow, or brown stone; sapphire, which is blue; emerald, which is often green; chalcedony, which can be blue or red; chrysoprase, which is green; beryl, which can be yellow or yellow–green; and topaz. Topaz is yellow and made up one of the higher foundations in the Revelation account of the city, though not the highest, as Kasey observed. It seems unbelievable that Kasey would describe all the colors of the City of God without having read Revelation previously, but I have no reason to doubt her.

Kasey's testimony reminds us that God hears silent as well as audible prayers, and it suggests that some people's prayers are particularly powerful. Kasey was able to hear a chorus of prayers when she stood before the Lord, and when she listened carefully she could distinguish between the voices. The two pastors who had visited her had prayed audibly by her side. She heard their words clearly. Her friend admitted to her that he had prayed for her silently, in the spirit, but when she was standing before God his prayers had also been audible. Her friend Stan's prayers had seemed "booming" in relation to the others. It makes me think of him as a prayer warrior, meaning one whose prayers are particularly strong. Consider James 5:16, which says, "The prayer of a righteous man is powerful and effective." The concept of a prayer warrior is elaborated in Ephesians 6:11–12: "Put on the full armor of God so that you can take your stand against the devil's schemes. For our struggle is not against flesh and blood, but against the rulers, against the authorities, against the powers of this dark world and against the spiritual forces of evil in the heavenly realms." These verses recall the earlier insights of Rev. Don Sweeting, who insisted that the power of prayer was influenced by the character of the person praying. He said:

> You need to be clean. You need to have your sins confessed if you're going to put yourself in this posi- tion. If you're going to be an instrument of God, to

bring comfort and healing to people, then you are a channel. I don't understand this exactly but somehow His work is in you and if you are unclean it gums up the works. There are a lot of prayer-busters, and that's one of them. You have to do business with God before you do this.[4]

Kasey was convinced that the prayers of her friends influenced God into restoring her health. This claim is backed up in James 5.

Is any one of you sick? He should call the elders of the church to pray over him and anoint him with oil in the name of the Lord. And the prayer offered in faith will make the sick person well; the Lord will raise him up. If he has sinned, he will be forgiven. Therefore confess your sins to each other and pray for each other so that you may be healed.

—James 5:14–16

Kasey was an exceptional patient. I do not mean that she was an easy patient to care for or that she cooperated placidly with my suggestions. Dr. Bernie Siegel, in his book *Love, Medicine, and Miracles*, describes some of the characteristics of patients who tend to get well and characteristics of those who don't.

People who always smile, never tell anyone their troubles, and neglect their own needs are the ones who are most likely to become ill....Physicians must realize that those patients who are difficult and stubborn are the ones most likely to get better. Aggressive patients who express their anger have more "killer T" cells.[5]

Kasey questioned all her doctors on every point. She demanded to be treated as a patient, not as a diagnosis. She wanted to know the side effects of every medication she was prescribed. I shall never forget the way she pointed her finger at me and reminded me, "You need to pray for all of your patients." As I mentioned before, the burden Kasey passed on to me, and which I humbly accept, is the job of speaking out in support of the power of prayer and the accuracy of the Bible. She had that rare conviction and sincerity evident in people who have endured mind-blasting ordeals but who nevertheless come out of their ordeals with a stronger faith and a deeper sense of purpose. Unlike many Christians and nonbelievers who struggle with doubts over the literal and symbolic meanings in the Bible, Kasey heard the prayers of her friends, she stood before the risen City of Jerusalem, and she stood before the very presence of God. Despite her major health problems, Kasey displayed the inner peace and assurance that very few people of superior health can match. Before her eventual death, Kasey knew that no matter what obstacles she encountered in this world, so long as she had faith, she could trust in the words of her friend with the booming voice, which can be found in Matthew 16:18: "On this rock I will build my church, and the gates of Hades will not overcome it."

CHAPTER 4

STEVE'S STORY: REJECTED BY GOD, THEN PEACE WITH GOD

Y NEXT PATIENT study includes a much more troubling near-death experience, but I believe it emphasizes the importance of a saving faith in God and developing and maintaining a personal relationship with Him. Steve was a 49-year-old, married, white male with a history of heart disease and prior heart attacks. He had undergone a previous heart bypass surgery and suffered from blocked arteries in his legs. He was admitted into the medical center with a new heart attack.

One morning I was at the hospital making rounds and preparing myself for an early meeting. While I was in the intensive care unit, Steve suffered a cardiac arrest. He was not one of my personal patients, but rather the patient of one of my partners. I ran to his room, where he was being resuscitated. There were 10 people there, including two doctors, several nurses, and one EKG technician, who was also a volunteer chaplain. I assumed the leadership role of the resuscitation team. I told the staff to charge up the defibrillator, and we shocked his heart back into a normal rhythm. Immediately Steve looked up at me in horror and panic, pointed at my right-hand side, pointed at the sky, and cried, "I'm not going up there!"

I asked, "What do you mean?"

He responded, "I saw Jesus standing next to you, and He wouldn't take me."

Here I was, having gone to the hospital that morning expecting to make rounds and go to a meeting, and now I was dealing with a horrified man who believed he had just been threatened with eternal damnation. My medical instructors had never prepared me for this!

I asked Steve what his religious background was, and he responded that he had been raised as a Southern Baptist but since adulthood had become inactive in his faith.

I said, "It's the easiest thing. Repent of your sins, accept Christ as your Lord and Savior, and follow the plan He has for your life." We prayed together right then, in front of the rest of the staff. But Steve was not out of the woods yet. For another hour or so he suffered recurrent cardiac arrests. Each time we shocked his heart back into a more stable rhythm, Steve had a similar look of horror and panic on his face. Steve finally stabilized and we sent him to the University Hospital to have a defibrillator–pacemaker inserted in hopes of keeping his heart rhythms normal, since we didn't have that particular pacemaker at our hospital.

Steve's wife was at medical center at that time, and I discussed her husband's situation with her. I told her that Steve was in a bad place, that he was suffering from both a medical and a spiritual crisis. Steve stayed at the hospital for around a week in stable condition but died on the following Sunday, which in addition to being Easter Sunday was the twenty-fifth wedding anniversary of him and his wife.

Afterwards I called his wife to comfort her and offer my condolences. She told me not to worry. She told me that Steve had died with peace in his heart, unafraid of where he was going. Something had happened to Steve during the week in which he was stable at the hospital. He had regained his faith and made peace with his God. His wife shared that on the morning of Easter Sunday, before he died, he and his wife had celebrated their anniversary.

Steve's story taught me many lessons: patients have bad as well as good near-death experiences, hell is a reality, and God holds us accountable for our lives.

On a more hopeful note, it is never too late to receive God's grace and make peace with Him. Something happened to Steve in the week before his death. He went from a non-practicing Christian to a committed believer, from a man traumatized by the reality of hell to a man at peace with the approach of his death. Steve's story also reminded me that Jesus is present alongside me, my staff, and my patients in trying circumstances, and I can take the burden off myself and rest assured that He is in charge. Steve's story reminds me that lives change for both the participants and the witnesses of these near-death experiences.

Most people don't want to hear about unpleasant near-death experiences. They want to believe that it's safe to die, that there is no such thing as judgment and hell, that near-death experiences involve encounters with compassionate, all-knowing lights, visions of heavenly splendors, and other positive images. But Christianity is a hard teaching in this secular world, and the Bible's messages concerning judgment are consistent, straightforward, and true.

Consider Matthew 7:13–14, where Jesus spoke about the way to heaven during His Sermon on the Mount speech: "Enter through the narrow gate. For wide is the gate and broad is the road that leads to destruction, and many enter through it. But small is the gate and narrow the road that leads to life, and only a few find it." Later Jesus says this about God's final judgment: "Then he will say to those on his left, 'Depart from me, you who are cursed, into the eternal fire prepared for the devil and his angels.'" God loves us, but He is a holy God and will hold people accountable for their sinfulness. However, He will also grant His gifts of grace and mercy to those with faith in Christ. In near-death experiences God can communicate these lessons.

The facts are that unpleasant near-death experiences are seldom reported for a variety of reasons. They may be suppressed or repressed. Doctors don't often interview patients who've had traumatic experiences, either because they want to respect the patient's privacy, they're uncomfortable with the subject, or because they don't believe near-death experiences deserve to be studied in the hard science of medicine. I believe these unpleasant visions are messages from God, in some cases reminding patients that their relationship with God must be improved. The message is also hopeful. God loves us and wants us to be closer to Him; and it is never too late to repent, to change our ways, and to accept His grace.

How is someone who is guilty redeemed? Can he do anything to make himself not guilty? No. As it says in Roman 3:10, "There is no one righteous, not even one." The only way he can become not guilty is by having his sins wiped away by Him who is able to say, "Your sins are forgiven. I paid the price."

Other doctors have reported negative near-death experiences. Dr. Maurice Rawlings is a cardiologist who has published several best-selling books, notably *Beyond Death's Door*, which partially deal with this subject. Dr. Rawlings has found that interviews immediately after patients are revived reveal as many bad experiences as good ones.[1]

As I mentioned, Steve had become inactive in his faith

before the last week of his life. Something profound took place in the last week of his life that allowed him to die at peace with the Lord, his faith renewed. This sort of transformation has a long history in the Bible. In the first chapter of the Book of Jonah, God commanded him to "go to the great city of Nineveh and preach against it, because its wickedness has come up before me" (v. 2). But Jonah ran away from this calling, unwilling to follow God's will. Instead of going to Nineveh, Jonah boarded a ship bound for another city. While on the ship, God's displeasure whipped the seas into a frenzy, convincing the sailors that someone on board was responsible for the crisis. Jonah admitted that he was running from God, and to save the sailors Jonah volunteered to be thrown into the sea. So they did so. But "the LORD provided a great fish to swallow Jonah, and Jonah was inside the fish three days and three nights" (Jonah 1:17). While there Jonah prayed to God for salvation, renewed his faith in Him, and vowed to accept God's plan for his life. After this, "The LORD commanded the fish, and it vomited Jonah onto dry land" (Jonah 2:10). Once on land Jonah preached to Nineveh as God had commanded, and he was forgiven.

Similarly, when Saul of Tarsus, later known as Paul, is first introduced in the book of Acts, he is ignoring God's plan for his life. He is persecuting and murdering Christians, including Stephen, a man full of God's grace and power, who "did great wonders and miraculous signs among the people" (Acts 6:8). Later, as Saul was traveling to Damascus to find Christians and return them as prisoners to Jerusalem, God intervened directly in his life.

> As he neared Damascus on his journey, suddenly a
> light from heaven flashed around him. He fell to the

ground and heard a voice say to him, "Saul, Saul, why do you persecute me?" "Who are you, Lord?" Saul asked. "I am Jesus, whom you are persecuting," he replied. "Now get up and go into the city, and you will be told what you must do." The men traveling with Saul stood there speechless; they heard the sound but did not see anyone. Saul got up from the ground, but when he opened his eyes he could see nothing. So they led him by the hand into Damascus. For three days he was blind, and did not eat or drink anything.

—Acts 9:3–9

Later, God told a man named Ananias to go to Saul and restore his sight, revealing his plan for Saul in the process.

"Go! This man is my chosen instrument to carry my name before the Gentiles and their kings and before the people of Israel. I will show him how much he must suffer for my name."

—Acts 9:15–16

When Ananias went to Saul, "something like scales fell from Saul's eyes, and he could see again. He got up and was baptized, and after taking some food, he regained his strength" (Acts 9:18–19). Saul immediately began preaching the good news of Christ all over the Roman Empire, becoming a great apostle. Like Jonah, he did not always heed God's plan for his life, but God kept seeking him, and eventually he accepted this plan.

I am not suggesting that Steve was an evil man before his transformation but merely that he had been far from God at that point. No matter what we do in our lives, no matter how our faith falters, it is never too late to repent and transform our lives.

Steve's experience affected the lives of the people who witnessed it. It gave me great assurance that Steve could see Jesus standing by my right-hand side. It is as if Steve was granted visual access to the spiritual realm that surrounds us at all times though we cannot always see it. As a fly fisherman, it makes me think of polarized glasses, which allows me to see fish through the water by cutting down on the sun's reflective glare. I wish everyone had the "spiritual glasses" Steve temporarily wore. As for me, it reminded me that I am not alone in my moments of need, dealing with life-and-death crises. In fact, it is when I am *most* in need that the Lord's presence can be felt most strongly. Patients suffering through medical tribulations should also be encouraged that they are not alone.

This experience also affected the lives of my staff. After Steve died I was giving a talk at the same medical center about the power of prayer. The audience was an assembly of chaplains. After I told Steve's story, the EKG technician and volunteer chaplain who had been present in the room stood up and confirmed the details of my story. Like me, she had been a Christian at the time, but the experience strengthened her belief that Jesus stays by our side. The chaplains in attendance, as well as my staff members who had been present for Steve's experience, were reminded that patients can have spiritual as well as medical crises and that prayer can go hand in hand with medical procedures in restoring a patient's well-being.

I'd like to share an experience Dr. Rawlings witnessed that echoes some of the lessons from Steve's story. Once Dr. Rawlings had a patient who had a cardiac arrest and dropped dead right in his office. He and his staff used heart compressions and mouth-to-mouth breathing techniques to try to revive him while the doctor attempted to insert a pacemaker. Here is part of that account from the bestselling book *Beyond Death's Door*:

> Each time he regained heartbeat and respiration, the patient screamed, "I am in hell!" He was terrified and pleaded with me to help him...He then issued a very strange plea: "Don't stop!" You see, the first thing most patients I resuscitate tell me, as soon as they recover consciousness, is "Take your hands off my chest; you're hurting me!"...But this patient was telling me, "Don't stop!"
>
> Then I noticed a genuinely alarmed look on his face. He had a terrified look worse than the expression seen in death! This patient had a grotesque grimace expressing sheer horror. His pupils were dilated, and he was perspiring and trembling...
>
> Then still another strange thing happened. He said, "Don't you understand? I am in hell. Each time you quit I go back to hell. Don't let me go back to hell!"
>
> Being accustomed to patients under this kind of emotional stress, I dismissed his complaint and told him to keep his "hell" to himself...
>
> But the man was serious, and it finally occurred to me that he was *indeed* in trouble... As a result, I started working feverishly and rapidly.
>
> By this time the patient had experienced three or four episodes of complete unconsciousness and clinical death...
>
> After several death episodes he finally asked me, "How do I stay out of hell?" I told him I guessed it

was the same principle learned in Sunday school—that I guessed Jesus Christ would be the one whom you would ask to save you.

Then he said, "I don't know how. Pray for me!"

Pray for him! What *nerve*! I told him I was a doctor, not a preacher.

"Pray for me!" he repeated.

I knew I had no choice. It was a dying man's request. So I had him repeat the words after me as we worked—right there on the floor. It was a very simple prayer because I did not know much about praying. It went something like this:

> *Lord Jesus, I ask you to keep me out of hell.*
> *Forgive my sins.*
> *I turn my life over to you.*
> *If I die, I want to go to heaven.*
> *If I live, I'll be "on the hook" forever.*

The patient's condition finally stabilized, and he was transported to a hospital. I went home, dusted off my Bible, and started reading it. I had to find out exactly what hell was supposed to be like. I had always dealt with death as a routine occurrence in my medical practice, regarding it as an extinction with no need for remorse or apprehension. Now I was convinced there was something about this life after death business after all. All my concepts needed revision. I needed to find out more. It was like finding another piece in the puzzle that supports the truth of the Scriptures. I was discovering the Bible was not merely a history book. Every word was turning out to be true. I decided I had better start reading it very closely.[2]

A few days later when Dr. Rawlings approached the man for an interview, he asked him what hell had been like. The man did not remember anything about hell, though he remembered the prayer. It seemed he had repressed all the unpleasant details! After the prayer, the patient's peace was restored, and his condition stabilized. Both Dr. Rawlings and his patient were transformed by this experience; both became committed Christians. The patient had only been an infrequent churchgoer before that time.

What changes people's hearts and brings them to repentance? As we've discussed, many people go through their lives believing that they don't need God, that they're self-reliant. When people are ill, their physical and emotional anguish, combined with their fear of death, puts cracks in this belief system and makes them more likely to give their burdens up to God. There's an urgent need for us to accept God's plan for us because we don't know when we're going to die and because the Bible teaches that hell is a place of no return. Not everyone will receive the warning signs that Steve did.

It is understandable why few negative near-death experiences are reported. Consider those who have seen a vision of hell and subsequently fear that hell is their destination. Sharing this belief with others must seem like the ultimate humiliation, a final judgment from God on their life and deeds. It's also the sort of admission that results in patients being considered crazy or unstable.

Dr. Rawlings believes that these experiences remind people of an unpleasant but necessary fact: everyone needs to get right with God, and not everyone is going to heaven. Many New Age thinkers teach that everyone goes to heaven. I also feel that many Christian churches deemphasize the reality of hell and the narrowness of the road to salvation.

In his book *To Hell and Back*, Dr. Rawlings discusses why some authors of near-death experience books don't report unpleasant experiences:

> Of course, some authors may not be happy about these cases, since negative experiences of any kind would prove embarrassing to a [philosophy] where everyone goes to heaven with no type of judgment involved.[3]

I believe this New Age philosophy that Dr. Rawlings mentions sounds appealing but is in fact dangerously misleading. Because of my faith, because of biblical teaching, because of my experiences with Steve and other patients, and based on reports I've heard from other doctors and medical staff, I believe that not all of us are going to the same place after our death. It is only through our faith in Him and by God's unmerited, amazing grace that we are saved.

CHAPTER 5

HOLY GROUND: THE ROOM OF THE DYING PATIENT

WHEN STEPPING INSIDE the room of a dying patient, I almost feel as if I should remove my shoes, for I consider it to be *holy ground*. God's presence is strong there. As always, He is seeking to develop or maintain relationships with everyone in the room, but especially the patients, whose souls hang in the balance. People are never more concerned about their relationship with God than when they are near death; it is understandably a setting for intense suffering, soul searching, and prayer.

This suffering, as Philip Yancey points out, can be a great equalizer, humbling us and refining our priorities, making us poor in spirit, and reminding us of our most central concerns: above all, our dependence on God and our need for redemption. In his book *Where Is God When It Hurts?* he quotes C. S. Lewis, who wrote that pain can be thought of as the megaphone of God.[1] It is one of His means of amplifying lessons we often are too self-sufficient to heed. It should be noted that each person's pain and suffering is equally important to God and equally important to His plan.

The dying room is also a place where many healing words are spoken; it is often the setting for reconciliation and forgiveness between family members and friends, and for intense bonding and pledges of love and support. It may be our last chance to get our lives in order before the next profound leg of our journey. Because it may be our last chance to settle accounts with our family, our friends, and our God, it becomes a place where the sacred replaces the mundane.

It is also understandably a place that is unpredictable and uncomfortable for most people. No one wants to go into the room of dying patients. Physicians, health care staff, chaplains, friends, and family of the patient do not feel comfortable there. It should be noted that physicians and chaplains receive little special training on how to come alongside patients in this situation, though most chaplains today are required to have completed a CPE (clinical pastoral education) program. Patients can be deeply angry and hostile toward their physician, family, or friends. They can be uncommunicative, inconsolable, and depressed. They can be in denial of their condition. They may bargain and plea with the physician to give them more time, somehow, regardless of how realistic their request is. As a result, most people don't want to be there, from physicians and nurses to chaplains, friends, and family. But it can also be the setting for miracles, especially when people accept the grace of God and place their trust in Him, allowing Him to shoulder the burden of their fear.

Working with these patients can be the most humbling part of a doctor's job. Because health care staff and chaplains receive little training in how to interact with patients in the dying room or with their families, they end up learning through difficult on the job experiences. These experiences may be humiliating and leave them with the sense that in the midst of such sacred work, they are somehow not measuring up to the gravity of the situation.

My friend, Dr. Dave Sorenson, whom I know from my Bible study group, experienced a duty in the U.S. Navy that mirrors this situation. He was stationed in Minneapolis after first serving onboard an aircraft carrier during the Vietnam War. One of his responsibilities was informing the parents and spouses of slain sailors about the deaths of their loved ones. Usually he went with one other officer, though sometimes he went alone. No one really taught him how to do this; he just learned on the job. He would be asked, "Are you a friend of my son?" or "Are you a friend of my husband?" and he would reply that he wasn't. The family members almost always fell apart and collapsed at this point. I asked Dave once how he got through those ordeals. He replied that the only reason he could handle those situations was that he had been born a preacher's kid. Since the time he was young he had known God was with him. In stressful times he maintained a state of constant, silent prayer. Whenever he visited a new set of parents or a spouse, he tried to create an atmosphere where they, too, would sense God's presence and take comfort from it. I share this goal when dealing with my patients.

But what do we do when we simply cannot comfort patients or their families, when they put up barriers we can't get through, when they don't trust us enough to confess their fears, their spiritual agonies, their financial worries, their disappointment with our care? In my experience, I've learned to trust silently through prayer in the dear Physician, the true Healer, that His will be done.

Before I share the stories of other patients and friends, I'll present a brief discussion of some of the stages of the dying patient. Elizabeth Kubler-Ross, MD, in her book *On Death and Dying*, explored this topic with great skill, sensitivity, and authority. She listed five common stages: denial and isolation, anger, bargaining, depression, and acceptance.[2]

When a patient is made aware of the severity of a terminal

disease or major illness, he or she often refuses to believe it. Sometimes, when I tell a patient that he is experiencing a heart attack, the patient will tell me he doesn't believe me. Since the first four hours after a heart attack are the most crucial hours in terms of caring for the patient, this can be a dangerous attitude.

Patients can also become very angry. They may direct their anger at their doctors and health care professionals, at their friends and families, or at God. They may accuse the doctors and nurses of misdiagnosing them. They may lash out at the habits of fellow patients in their vicinity.

Dr. Kubler-Ross calls the third stage the bargaining stage. At this stage, patients often make private or overt deals with their doctors or with God, seeking some sort of remedy for their pain and fear. Dr. Kubler-Ross writes:

> Most bargains are made with God and are usually kept secret or mentioned between the lines in a chaplain's private office. There are many who promise a life dedicated to God or a life in the service of the church in exchange for some additional time. Many also promise to give their bodies to science.[3]

I've had patients ask me to keep them alive long enough to meet their grandchildren. I've had patients beg me for more life. As you may recall, my patient Kasey asked God for 10 more years of life so she could be with her family and share her story with others.

In the fourth stage, patients often get depressed. Their anger turns inwards. They may become hopeless about their chances of survival, they may blame their own lifestyle choices for their illness, and they may become despondent and uncommunicative. The rigors of surgeries, procedures, medications, and pain may simply overwhelm them, not to mention the concerns about the financial cost of their treatment and the burdens they are placing on their family.

In the last stage, patients usually come to accept their illness. Dr. Kubler-Ross writes:

> Acceptance should not be mistaken for a happy stage. It is almost void of feelings. It is as if the pain had gone, the struggle is over, and there comes a time for "the long rest before the journey," as one patient phrased it. This is also the time in which the family usually needs more help, understanding, and support than the patient himself.[4]

I should note that this can also be a stage of great peace compared to the more agonizing stages of depression and anger. Once, at the end of my day, I visited a woman who was dying of cancer and had developed some cardiac arrhythmias. I did not want to be there; I was tired and ready to go home. I walked in and took a history of her problems and performed a physical examination. Her peace and acceptance were truly inspiring and healing to me. This is not a rare occurrence. I left her feeling as if she should have handed me a bill for lifting my spirits and encouraging me. I was touched by her peacefulness.

Dr. Kubler-Ross writes that there are many reasons why these stages can be so full of agony:

> Dying nowadays is more gruesome in many ways, namely, more lonely, mechanical, and dehumanized; at times it is even difficult to determine technically when the time of death has occurred....He may cry for rest, peace and dignity, but he will get infusions,

transfusions, a heart machine, or a tracheotomy if necessary. He may want one single person to stop for one single second so that he can ask one single question.[5]

After interviewing many patients, Dr. Kubler-Ross made several useful conclusions. Patients said that when doctors first broke the news about their illness, "It was the sense of empathy which counted more than the immediate tragedy of the news."[6] This is further evidence that patients do not want to be treated as just another number to be shuffled through as quickly as possible. Other patients told Dr. Kubler-Ross that what grieved them the most during their illness was the loss of hope. Even when the news is grim, doctors should not make the situation sound hopeless. Dr. Kubler-Ross claims there is "an art to sharing the news of dying with a patient."[7] Patients want to hear the reassurance that everything possible will be done, that they will not be "dropped," that there are treatments available, that there is a glimpse of hope—even in the most advanced cases.[8]

She developed this idea further later on:

> This doesn't mean the doctors told them a lie, but they want doctors to share with them the idea that something unforeseen may happen, that they may have a remission, that God may intervene, that they will live longer than expected. If a patient stops expressing hope it is usually a sign of impending death.[9]

Dr. Kubler-Ross also pointed out that patients do not want doctors to always avoid talking about the possibility of them dying. Many patients are morbidly depressed until we broach the subject of their deaths. I am convinced we do more damage by avoiding the issue than by taking time to sit, listen, and share.[10]

As I said in the first chapter, doctors should always leave the patient with some measure of hope. As many of the stories in this book demonstrate, regarding the reality of the afterlife and the presence of Christ by our side, there is much to be hopeful about, even when one's physical prognosis is grim. Dr. Kubler-Ross's other insights regarding empathy and the importance of caregivers taking the time to listen to patients are also crucial and will be discussed further in the later chapter regarding patient advocacy.

I will now share some of the stories of friends I've had whose experiences in the dying room are instructive. The story of Karyl and his wife Patty illustrates, among other things, how the family members of patients should give patients "permission" to die. Often patients feel guilty for their illness; they feel they are disappointing or even failing their loved ones by dying. Sometimes these feelings are not communicated. This story also shows how patients can find peace more quickly when their family members are willing to communicate about their deepest fears. It also shows how a patient's faith can inspire family members to renew their own relationships with God.

Patty enjoyed periods of good health up until a month or so before she died. In her last month her cancer rapidly advanced, and she deteriorated quickly, sparing her and her family the anguish of a long, drawn-out death. During the periods of good health she was able to spend much quality time with her loved ones. Previous to her good periods she had received a bone marrow transplant, which ultimately failed to help her physically, though it had made her hopeful for recovery. She had also received intensive chemotherapy and radiation. Patty's death was made easier by an exceptionally loving community. Her husband Karyl, a physician, recalled:

> I was extremely fortunate during that time to have so many physicians among the many neighbors and friends who were with us. So many people lifted the burden of responsibility from my shoulders and took turns supervising. That gave me the chance to spend more time with my children and my other family members. With the exception of nighttime activities, Patty's dying room was almost never empty. Someone was with her round-the-clock. I could leave the room and go hop into the bunk bed and get some sleep and then be re-energized to a certain extent.[11]

Most people do not have such intensive, round-the-clock support, especially from a crowd made up partly of physicians. Anytime the burdens of care can be passed around, the quality of the patient interaction increases. Karyl recalled that the presence of music also contributed to a soothing atmosphere. The soundtrack to the film *Out of Africa*, he remembered, was almost always on and gave Patty great comfort.

During Patty's lucid moments she was able to be open with Karyl about her concerns for the family's future and her reflections about their life together. The "Holly" referred to in this quote from Karyl refers to the woman who became Karyl's future wife after Patty's death.

Some of these periods were spent talking about the future and one of those discussions was oriented around who Patty thought I should marry. She was absolutely convinced this female minister she knew was the right choice. I wasn't going to argue with her in the throes of dying. If she would have met Holly before, I'm sure she would have been at the top of her list. I wish that I had an opportunity to have those conversations back to replay them. We talked about heaven, we talked about our life, we talked about what she expected with the kids, and what she expected for their education. We talked about trying to communicate after she was dead; we tried to make assurances that we would find each other when we were both in heaven. That provided a sense of comfort for both of us. I also tried to reassure her that she'd meet up in heaven with other family members. I remember trying to reassure her that everything she wanted would be done. I think that there must be a lot of guilt associated with dying; the dying person is frustrated about unfinished tasks and projects. By dying they've lost their ability to pay tribute to their families. It's a dehumanizing process to take that role of responsibility away from someone. They can no longer contribute to the family financially through their job, and they can no longer contribute as a parent. I was struck at that moment by how important it was to be able to say, "Don't worry about it." Because it's very important to explicitly tell that person that everything is going to be OK; it gives them the ability to let go.[12]

One day I went to visit Patty and was sitting on one side of her bed, holding her hand, with her sister on the other side of

the bed. Patty was in a state of stupor. She regained conscious-
ness and looked at me and looked confused. People frequently
tell Karyl and me that we look alike; our mustaches and facial
structures are similar. I quickly got off the bed since she was
looking for Karyl, and brought Karyl to the bedside, where
he talked with her. Patty asked Karyl if she was dying. He
said, "Yes, but you've done everything right." I will always
cherish the memory of this profoundly tender moment. Karyl
was giving her permission to die by assuring her there was
nothing more she had to worry about. Later Karyl questioned
the idea some people have that dying silently and unexpect-
edly in one's sleep is the best way to die:

> When someone dies suddenly the chance to really
> process with them, forgive them, thank them, and to
> help plan with them are ripped from you. We often
> speak as doctors, having seen so much suffering,
> about how cruel it would be to have a long-term
> illness. We say, "So-and-so died suddenly in his sleep
> and that's the way to go." That may be the way you
> want to go from a suffering aspect, but maybe not in
> the sense of how it will affect the family.[13]

Karyl also spoke of how his experience with Patty's illness
helped give him a new perspective and how that perspective,
along with the faith of his new wife, led him toward a deeper
commitment to God.

> I remember when Patty was sick it was hard to listen to
> people with their mundane concerns and complaints.
> An experience like that gives you a chance to reflect
> upon your life. Then I met Holly and had an oppor-
> tunity for a new life. *Walking to Higher Ground*, so

to speak, *is achieved only through taking baby steps.* And my experiences with life and to a greater extent Patty's illnesses and death helped put together the stairway to be able to get to higher ground. And I don't hold myself out as a pinnacle at this point in time, but I'm certainly able to have a more meaningful relationship with Christ than I did before. I used to be more of a Sunday-morning Christian, but I didn't bring it into the fabric of my day-to-day life. I learned that is not the sort of behavior that's associated with having a more enriching relationship with God. And I think that my observations and my experiences helped create the background for taking this step, which was meeting Holly and getting involved in my church and accepting Christ into my life. Now I'm more actively seeking the Word and communicating with Christ. Before it was superficial, but later Holly was most responsible for helping me take that next step.[14]

Patty's dying room was in many ways ideal. There was an active, loving community of people sharing the burdens of care. She was able to express her many concerns about her family's future, from the choice of a wife for her husband to the welfare of her children. Her husband reassured her that she had done everything right. In short, she was able to put all her worldly affairs in order and rest easy that her previous responsibilities were now in good hands.

Diane's story illustrates how it is never too late for the power of forgiveness to affect the quality of a patient's last days. Diane and her husband, Don, had four sons. When two of the sons were in college and two in high school, Diane and Don separated, against Diane's will, because of various violations in their marriage covenant. Diane had had a strong faith in God since before their marriage, and she believed that marriage vows were permanent, so she kept trying to stay in contact with Don. She told me:

> We never lost touch with each other, and our love was still there in spite of everything that happened. I believed that marriage is insoluble, and he felt that too; that's part of our faith. We were still together on family occasions. But it wasn't quite the same. We tried to get back together several times, but it was just like this difference had taken place. So my faith is always what I've relied on and it has just become stronger and stronger.[15]

At times during their separation Diane became very angry with Don. At one point Diane read about how the Blessed Mother had been appearing in a small village named Medjugorje in Bosnia, Herzegovina. This spoke to her heart, Diane told me, and she decided she had to go. While in confession there, a priest told her that she must pray for Don and forgive him. She realized she had been praying for her own welfare but not for his. She told me:

> It was just like magic. The anger went away. I came back and said to Don, "I'd really like to ask for your forgiveness for anything I've done to hurt you, and I forgive you." He just started to cry.[16]

About five years after her trip to Europe, Don developed lung cancer. He underwent radiation therapy and chemotherapy. He then developed drug-induced Parkinson's disease. His cancer eventually spread to his brain, which killed him.

When Don discovered he had cancer, he asked Diane to accompany him to his treatment. Diane considered the decision to be a no-brainer, and she agreed to go with him. At that point they hadn't yet moved back in together. Slowly they healed their relationship. Diane went back for confession in Europe three more times. Eventually Don joined her for one of the trips. Soon they moved back in together and renewed their wedding vows in the presence of their children. Diane felt great peace. She told me why she believed the relationship was healed:

> I would pray, "This is how I'd like it to be." I'd always wanted to forgive Don my way. I had taken control instead of God. Finally I began praying the way God wanted, which was praying for Don. Before we reconciled, I didn't know why we couldn't work things out; we weren't letting God do it. It was God that put us together again. We feel like we have to control everything, and it was about submitting to Him and saying this is a bigger problem than we can handle. And He did take care of it when we asked.[17]

The reconciliation, according to Diane, had positive effects on their sons and their immediate families. Jesus makes it clear in the Bible that we must forgive each other. In Matthew 6:14–15 Jesus says, "For if you forgive men when they sin against you, your heavenly Father will also forgive you. But if you do not forgive men their sins, your Father will not forgive your sins." This concept often goes against our natural instincts about what people deserve. In America we are saturated with the concept of justice. Great importance is placed on punishing criminals in proportion to their crimes. God teaches us that it is not our place to do the punishing;

it is His responsibility. It is our duty to forgive, recognizing that we are all sinners, and that it is only through the grace of God that we are saved. When people ask me how I'm doing, I often say, "Better than I deserve." Without God's grace, I would be in trouble, for like all people, I am fallen. I am a sinner saved by grace. To quote Jesus again, from Matthew 7:3, "Why do you look at the speck of sawdust in your brother's eye and pay no attention to the plank in your own eye?" Diane forgave her husband, received his forgiveness in turn, and helped to reconcile the family before his death.

The story of my friend Chuck details another situation that was ideal in many ways. When his father was dying at Chuck's home, the extended family was present, the father talked openly about the afterlife and the settling of his financial affairs, and people were able to freely express their love for each other and their concerns about the future. The story also discusses the idea of a "special kind of brokenness." This concept refers to a state people find themselves in when the normal boundaries people put up made of pride, self-sufficiency, fear, or insecurities, are broken down. This can happen as the result of the calming presence of God's grace. In such moments loved ones interact with rare honesty and openness. In these moments, God's grace is flowing through His created instruments.

Chuck's father, Leslie, was a hero to his son and many of his family members and friends. Leslie was the oldest of many children and had assumed the role of patriarch within the family as a result of his hard work, generosity, and devotion to family and friends. When he first got married, he and his wife lived in a one-room dugout with a dirt floor. They slept with washcloths over their faces to keep the debris raised by Great Plains dust storms out of their mouths and noses. A thoroughly self-made man, he ended up being a successful business owner and devoted father of two children.

When Leslie came out to Colorado for the last time to visit me professionally, he told Chuck how he wanted the family business and finances to be taken care of after he was gone. Chuck reassured his father that he was not going to die and that they could discuss these matters later, though he was troubled by how confident his father seemed regarding his approaching death.

While Leslie was in Denver he was admitted to the hospital with congestive heart failure. One day I was walking the halls in the hospital where Leslie was staying. I ran into Chuck as he was going to his father's room. He was trying hard to be the leader of the family during that ordeal and assume the patriarchal role his father had always handled with such authority. One of Chuck's major sources of motivation had always been the desire to live up to his father's expectations, and I could tell that he was struggling. I told Chuck in the hospital hallway that it was all right for him to be his dad's boy.

After these words, Chuck broke down and wept. We embraced together in the hospital hallway. Chuck told me later that these words "gave me permission to cry and permission to feel. It made me feel like I didn't have to be in charge of everything. For you and me it was a transformation of our relationship; we were realizing we were in the presence of the Lord."[18]

We decided to move Leslie into Chuck's home for his final days. Leslie's entire family came to visit with him. Leslie talked at length with Chuck and the others about his curiosity regarding heaven. He wanted to know what it would really look like and how it would make him feel. Chuck told me:

I've always felt that most Christians have moments when they wake up and think, "Is heaven just a myth?" When my father asked me those questions, it was a real test of my faith. It was a situation where I had to tell myself, "This is it. What do you really believe?" And from that day forward, I never doubted again.[19]

Chuck remembered asking me at one point what else he could do to comfort his father. I told him that he had to give his father permission to die. At one point, soon before his death, Leslie began speaking about how he wanted his business and finances to be handled, as he had before. This time, instead of protesting that he could worry about that later, Chuck began writing his father's words down. He felt as if a baton was now being passed to him. He also remembered his father saying, "You will be fine. Take care of your mother, and take care of your family. You've been a very good son, and I hope I have been a good father."[20] Chuck told me that he knew at that point that his father would die that night. And he did, after everyone had gone to sleep except Leslie's wife. Chuck believed it had always been his father's intentions to die that way.

Chuck remembered that his daughter, Kara, had been afraid to approach Leslie at this time. Leslie had always seemed a pillar of strength to her, as he had for the rest of the family, and it was particularly difficult for her to imagine him being gone. Also, it was her high school graduation at that time, and though she never admitted it openly, Chuck believed she was upset that she couldn't enjoy her graduation like she wanted to. Eventually, however, she came alongside her grandfather and listened to him talk about heaven and his hopes for her.

Chuck believes her faith became much stronger at this time, partially because she felt how strong God's presence was in the dying room, a presence so strong Chuck described the room of his father's bed as "hallowed ground."[21]

Chuck also told me that he felt a "special kind of broken-ness"[22] during the deaths of certain family members. Boundaries were broken; people became comfortable in each other's presence regardless of how humiliating the situations might have normally been. Chuck remembered how his father had always wanted to be well groomed. As a result, Leslie asked Chuck to shave him and cut his hair each day. Moments like this, and the moment when Chuck felt he could just be his "dad's boy," are crucial in making the dying process as open, loving, and comfortable as possible.

The next story I will share does not take place in the context of a dying room in America but in the infamous Killing Fields of Cambodia. It is a powerful testament to the power of forgiveness. Reverend Setan Lee is a giant of a man, a minister who has devoted much of his life to bringing the word of Christ to the people of Cambodia. I have known Setan through my experiences in the Christian Medical Ministry to Cambodia/Jeremiah's Hope (www.cmmcjh.com).

From 1975 to 1979 Setan lived in a concentration camp in Cambodia under the authority of the Khmer Rouge.[23] The Khmer Rouge was a Communist group that had been rounding up and slaughtering all educated people from all disciplines, Christians, and non-Christian religious leaders in the most massive genocidal movement of the last 35 years, often referred to as the Killing Fields. William F. Buckley Jr, founder of the magazine *National Review*, estimated that the Khmer Rouge wiped out around 2 million people in the 1970s out of a population of 7 million.[24] While in the concentration camp the prisoners lived in abysmal conditions, suffered torture, and carried out brutal slave labor, frequently dropping from fatigue to die where they fell. One day, while Setan was laboring beside a female friend, his friend brushed a small crayfish towards him for him to eat. A female guard noticed this. She promptly came over and placed a plastic bag over the head of his friend and strangled her to death on the spot. They then placed Setan up to his neck in an anthill, expecting this to kill him. But he lived. Later during his captivity, they found his college identification on his person and promptly brought him to a place to be executed. As several of his fellow prisoners were clubbed to death in front of him, he prayed to the God of the universe to save his life and promised to bear witness to God afterwards. At the last second his life was spared. In 1979 Setan escaped the Killing Fields by running through the jungle on dead men's bones to avoid landmines. He found himself alone in the jungle. He told me he was at this time a man "full of the spirit of revenge, a man full of anger, a man full of desperation."[25]

While in the jungle he met a wild man who was evangelizing for Christ. This man spoke to Setan about the good news of the gospel. Setan received Christ into his heart that day. He told me how this affected his spirit of revenge:

> When I received Christ as my Lord and Savior all those things supernaturally disappeared from me, and instead I just felt compassion and love and mercy toward those people who don't know the Lord and who have not experienced what I have experienced.[26]

Setan escaped from the jungle after much hardship and became a preacher and a Bible teacher. He became a pastor at a church for refugees from the Killing Fields.

One day, while he was preaching in a Thailand refugee camp, he noticed that the female guard who had killed his female friend was in his church. His first instinct was to break her neck. He told me:

> I hated her. I thought to myself, "There is no 30-step plan I can follow to forgive her." But when God gave me the supernatural power to forgive her, it was all I needed. It's just one step. If I go to the Lord and surrender everything to Him I can forgive not only the lady but the rest of the Khmer Rouge in Cambodia.[27]

Setan left his position of preaching and went down and knelt before this woman and asked her to forgive him for the hatred he felt toward her. Not only had Setan forgiven this woman, he was asking this woman to forgive him. This was clearly an example of divine love and forgiveness. He told her that Jesus loves her and so does he.

Eventually he came to America, where he could formulate plans for spreading the Word of God in Cambodia. He has now been working as a pastor in Cambodia since 1990. Sometimes when he goes back he preaches forgiveness to former Khmer Rouge members who remain in the country. In fact, several of his deputy pastors are former Khmer Rouge generals. On one of these missions in 2002, in which he was to speak before 35,000 former Khmer Rouge, he had to go many miles by foot through the jungle to reach their camp. It was very dangerous, and he became very sick for a while as a result. But he was and is driven to forgive his former captors and the oppressors of his countrymen. He has said that many of the Khmer Rouge are wracked with guilt. Yet he, of all people, has compassion for them.

Setan has said, "When you forgive someone it's not just that person who benefits, because you yourself are the one who is set free."[28] He also points out that we must forgive ourselves if we expect to forgive others. For some people, this step is more difficult than pardoning others. But as the Bible commands us in Matthew 22:39, "Love your neighbor as yourself."

Setan's story took place far from the setting of the hospital, but it nevertheless demonstrates that with God by our side, no crime we suffer should be beyond our power to forgive. If Setan was able to forgive the murderer of his family and the people who perpetuated genocide against his homeland, we can certainly forgive the people who disappoint us in our own lives. Such forgiveness can make the dying room a holy place. God's presence is strong, and when there is a strong community of supportive people, along with a health care staff that gives patients hope, an atmosphere can be created in which God can work miracles in people's lives. The dying room is not merely where patients spend their last moments alive. It is the climax of their spiritual lives, where the state of their relationship with God takes center stage.

These stories also involve the transformative effects of intense suffering. None of us shall escape suffering in this life, but such suffering, as Philip Yancey points out in his book *Where Is God When It Hurts?* can have "advantages." In our heated homes, within our gated walls, in our speedy cars that bypass slums, with our planes that lift us above war and strife, with our medical care that shields us from disease, with our anesthesia that numbs the pain of sliced nerves during surgeries, we may more easily fall into the illusion that we don't need

God. But as Yancey says, "Those who suffer can respond to the call of the gospel with a certain abandonment and uncomplicated totality because they have so little to lose and are ready for anything."[29] Suffering can make clear what is less essential, like our attachments to worldly possessions, to luxuries, to sin, to exaggerated fears, to superficial or false friendships, to meaningless pursuits.

As in Chuck's story, suffering can facilitate the "special brokenness" that brings us back to a "dependent humility on God." As it says in Psalm 51, what pleases God is "a broken spirit, a broken and contrite heart" (v. 17). This brokenness can often be God's way to teach, discipline, and refine us by reminding us of what is essential to our lives, like our relationships with our friends, family, and God. Saints who have so little in the way of worldly comfort are more in tune with these essentials. Yancey emphasizes, "Dependence, humility, simplicity, cooperation, abandon—these are qualities greatly prized in the spiritual life, but extremely elusive for those who live in comfort."[30]

An understanding of this state of dependence can be enlarged by considering the concept of being "poor in spirit." "Blessed are the poor in spirit," as Jesus says in the first Beatitude on the Sermon on the Mount (Matt. 5:3). To be poor in spirit is to realize one's need for God. It is an attitude similar to the dependent humility upon God that E. M. Bounds says we should aspire to during prayer. As Dr. David Martyn Lloyd-Jones says, "It does not imply material poverty and does not imply weakness of character."[31] It does not mean we need to sell our homes and wander in rags. It does not mean that we are *spiritless*, that we should shrink from hardship or fail to take bold action. It involves the emptying of one's self, of one's pride, of our selfishness and worldly distractions so that we may be filled back up by God. It can also be viewed as breaking ourselves apart like a piece of pottery so that God may put us back together with a clay made of Holy Spirit.

How do we become poor in Spirit? According to Dr. Lloyd-Jones, we first must look at Jesus, which will make us realize our "absolute poverty and emptiness." Viewing Christ's supremacy makes us recognize our illusions of self-reliance. Secondly, we repent. As Jones says, "We turn away from our independence of spirit and humble ourselves before God. It is the starting point for the renewal of our minds."[32] Like the revolutionary teachings of the Sermon on the Mount, it is a radical process of re-learning after the influence of worldly values, such as the pressure to be free from all restraint, free to "do it our way."

The poor in spirit are often those in extreme poverty, the oppressed, the helpless, and the marginalized, such as those confined with Setan Lee in the Killing Fields or those "crying out to God,"as Dr. Jim Dixon shares in his sermons on the subject.[33] They are the spiritually humble, who seek their security in God alone. Philip Yancey adds that they "can respond to the call of the Gospels with a certain abandonment and uncomplicated totality because they have so little to lose and are ready for anything."[34] From their experience of poverty, they are in a better position to understand the Gospels. It might seem to us as though people with the leisure and opportunity to study the Scriptures and theology should understand the Gospels better than the uneducated poor, yet the experience of deprivation and poverty, and the special brokenness that comes along with that, transcend the lessons to be gained from book learning. We are reminded of Christ's own suffering when we see people who have no shelter against catastrophe, when we see the hundreds of thousands of refugees created by Hurricane Katrina, to give but one example. As Sister Monika Hellwig, a nun and professor of theology, says, "The memory of Christ is present in every hungry, thirsty, oppressed and humiliated person."[35]

Furthermore, the oppressed remind us painfully of the costs of sinfulness, since we must examine how greed, injustice, violence, and cruelty have consequences that last for generations, as we see in the Killing Fields of Cambodia. We can hardly expect Setan Lee to easily forget the costs of genocide, labor camps, and war—man's potential for inhumanity toward man.

Chuck's story gives a more local example of the advantages of being broken in spirit. Through this brokenness, he was able to be his father's son and cement his relationship with his father before his father died. Setan Lee experienced suffering that most Americans are sheltered from; he witnessed survivors of the Killing Fields so poor in spirit that everyone who comes in contact with them will never forget them. The lessons Setan took from his own suffering, and the suffering of his countrymen, are main reasons why he is a giant among pastors in terms of the conviction of his teachings.

Yet when it comes to suffering, Christ provides the ultimate example, and following His example brings us honor before God. It is important to note that just because we suffer doesn't mean we are sanctified. Pastor Brian Myers from the Dillon Community Church in Dillon, Colorado, adds insight on this subject in the following teaching, which draws from 1 Peter 1:18-25.

> How is it to your credit if you receive a beating for doing wrong and endure it? But if you suffer for doing good and you endure it, this is commendable

before God. To this you were called, because Christ suffered for you, leaving you an example that you should follow in his steps. 'He committed no sin, and no deceit was found in his mouth.' When they hurled their insults at him, he did not retaliate; when he suffered, he made no threats. *Instead, he entrusted himself to Him who judges justly.* He himself bore our sins in his body on the tree, so that we might die to sins and live for righteousness; by his wounds you have been healed. For you were like sheep going astray, but now you have returned to the Shepherd and Overseer of your souls.[36] [emphasis added]

Pastor Myers teaches that we must bear our suffering like a man or woman of God and come to God as a child, open and receptive, full of reverential trust. Similarly, a teaching of St. Peter gave me much comfort when I recently was suffering from a herniated cervical disc, and also when I see suffering in my patients and friends. St. Peter states in 1 Peter 4:19, "So then, those who suffer according to God's will should commit themselves to their faithful Creator and continue to do good." We should not get off the train of our life journey when the going gets tough or difficult. We should not stop doing what He has called us to do but "run with perseverance the race marked out for us" (Heb. 12:1).

On the subject of forgiveness, Pastor Myers went on to say that bitterness is the poison we swallow when hoping the other person will die. Bitterness makes you into the victim. Forgiveness, however, makes you be the man or woman God chooses you to become. Forgiveness turns you into the victor.[37]

In both Setan's and Diane's stories, their forgiveness turned them into victors. How easy would it have been for Setan to stay embittered toward the woman captor who had killed his friend? How could Diane have aided and loved her husband when he was dying if she had remained angry and hardened by the violations in their past?

The dying room, as we have seen, is a holy place, the last station before our departure into death. There we no longer have time to worry about inconsequential matters. It is a place of intense suffering and humility, a place of reconciliation and forgiveness, a place where a "special brokenness" makes people express themselves in their most genuine, heartfelt way. It is a place where we may become poor in spirit and thus more receptive to the "megaphone of God," to those lessons we may have shirked during good times. Above all, it is our last chance to express our dependence on God's grace, our total trust in His plan for our lives, and our total trust on His plan for our afterlife. Our ultimate healing will occur when we each come into His eternal presence.

CHAPTER 6

DIVINE EXPERIENCES: VISIONS AND VISITATIONS FROM GOD

S OMETIMES THE DIVINE Spirit or angelic beings reveal themselves to people in everyday life. While these occurrences don't happen to everyone and don't happen all the time, I firmly believe that they *do* happen. Some of my patients have had divine experiences, as have some of my friends and medical associates. I believe the purpose of divine experiences is to comfort people, give them hope, and remind them that God wants a relationship with them and that His grace is available to everyone. At the same time, we should be cautious about accepting every account of a divine experience as an actual visitation by God or one of His angels. This is because many Christian thinkers believe that the devil also reveals himself to people to deceive them, tempt them, and lead them astray; he masquerades as an agent of the light. Of course, some people's accounts of divine experiences are only hallucinations or lies or visions produced by altered states. Often when I share the experiences I'm about to relate, members of my audience come forward and speak of similar experiences. I hope the following stories remind people of the many ways God wants to comfort us and transform us by His saving grace.

The first story I will relate concerns a patient of mine named Merl, who considers himself to be a "blue-collar Christian."[1] He describes himself that way because of his humble origins;

his hard-drinking, hard-living lifestyle in the navy; and his long career in an unglamorous job, a job often held in low esteem by others. Merl entered the navy at the age of 17, where he got the first of many tattoos that would eventually cover his body. Years of hard living took a toll on his body, and he developed heart disease at an early age. He spent much of his career working as an environmental services worker in Denver hospitals. By the time he was 41 he underwent his first coronary artery bypass surgery. Fifteen years later doctors performed a second coronary artery bypass operation. In 2001 a stent was placed in one of his coronary arteries. A year later, I attempted to insert four more stents into one of his coronary arteries. I told him before we started that there was about a 50 percent chance he would experience a heart attack during the procedure.

When I recently interviewed Merl, he told me that he had been praying before and during the procedure and that many of his friends and family members had been praying for him. Before previous procedures and surgeries Merl had been tense; this time, he said he'd never felt so relaxed in his life. During the procedure, Merl remembers I was having some difficulty inserting the last of the four stents. Here is Merl's account of what happened next.

> You turned around and told your assistant to get a different brand of stent. Meanwhile I was lying there praying, and I suddenly saw this "being" standing over your left shoulder, just observing what was going on. He was only there for a few moments. As you worked, suddenly he reached out and put his hand on your shoulder. At that instant I remember you said, "I just inserted the last stent." Immediately the figure vanished.[2]

Merl had not been on any drugs that would have disoriented him, impaired his sight, or increased the chances that he would hallucinate. Merl added that the figure was dressed in a white robe, with shoulder-length hair. He was beardless, clean-cut, and seemed to have the calm, dignified presence of a holy person. He did not have wings. Although Merl had been more calm than usual during the procedure, seeing the figure added an enormous amount of reassurance. Merl felt a renewed sense that God was in charge of the procedure, and furthermore, that God had a definite plan for Merl's life after the procedure.

In the hustle and bustle of the staff following the insertion of the stent, Merl didn't feel that the time was right to share his experience. Within a month, however, during an office visit, Merl did share what had happened. He told me that he felt like a new man. He felt driven to fulfill God's plan for his life. Specifically, one of Merl's five children had largely followed in Merl's footsteps when it came to leading a rowdy lifestyle. Merl felt God wanted him to help his troubled son seek to develop a relationship with God, and he was committed to this pursuit when I saw him. Merl told me:

> I'm kind of a hard-headed old guy. God has a purpose for me. I do feel he's keeping me around for something. I have felt for some time that he may be keeping me around to help my kids, especially one of my sons, who is as wild as I ever was.[3]

When I heard Merl's story I gathered the members of the hospital staff who had been present during Merl's experience to share with them what had happened. Some were unsettled by his account; many, like me, felt great reassurance at the news.

I will never forget inserting that stent; Merl's experience has made that procedure one of my most inspiring and encouraging memories. Sometimes when I am in the middle of difficult medical procedures I feel like I'm standing in mud, and a heavy burden settles over my shoulders. I may feel the pressure to save a life; I may feel the worried eyes of a patient's family and friends staring through the walls. All physicians have moments when the tools of their profession are inadequate, when all their skills cannot slow the decline of a patient's health, when all their knowledge sheds no light on the mysteries of illness. Testimonies like Merl's remind me that I am not ultimately in charge of the patient's outcome. In my most stressful moments I am reminded that I can take my load off, give it to the Lord, and say "Lord, You guide me. You take charge and carry the load."

Merl's story makes me recall an early episode in my own medical career when I had doubts about my own practice. In April 1987 I was performing the fourth angioplasty of my career. Performing an angioplasty involves inflating a balloon inside an artery to open up a blocked passage. In 1987 the success rate for angioplasties was less than 90 percent, and the complication rate was between 7 and 10 percent. On that occasion my patient had a tight narrowing in the artery at the front of his heart. When I inflated the balloon, his artery immediately closed off! At that time stents were not yet used to keep the passage open. My only option was to have the patient undergo an emergency bypass surgery. I called a heart surgeon to perform the surgery. By the time the doctor moved my patient into the operating room, his heart had stopped, and cardio-pulmonary resuscitation (CPR) was being applied. That's how my patient left my care. I was devastated. I felt that what I had to offer as a physician to this patient was inadequate and that this patient was fighting for his life. Was God trying to tell me that I shouldn't perform this new procedure? Was I putting my patients through unnecessary risks?

I immediately prayed deeply about these questions. I called several of my prayer partners, as well as my church prayer chain, to pray for this patient. Fortunately, my patient made a full recovery and was discharged in improved health with no permanent damages from his cardiac arrest. Experiences like this, in which one's skills feel inadequate, are common among physicians and health care workers. We will never have the expertise and equipment to protect our patients from every encounter with illness and death. We must recognize our limitations and resist the urge to allow our successes to make us feel as if we are solely responsible for the health of our patients. God may use us as His instruments of healing, but He is ultimately in charge. And, as we've mentioned before, the passage from life to death does not always signal a defeat in a patient's life. For many it is a triumphant, transcendent occasion, worthy of joy. When physicians and health care workers feel overburdened, I urge them to give their burden to God. They should do their best but keep a healthy perspective on who is really in charge of the situation.

Merl's experience transformed his life and reminded me and some of my staff members about the presence of God at all times in our lives, whether it be a medical crisis or a crisis in our home life. As we mentioned in the last chapter, God is always seeking us, wanting us to surrender to Him and pass our burdens onto His shoulders. As it says in Matthew 11:28–30:

Come to me, all you who are weary and burdened, and I will give you rest. Take my yoke upon you and learn from me, for I am gentle and humble in heart, and you will find rest for your souls. For my yoke is easy and my burden is light.

These verses teach that "Jesus promises love, healing and peace with God, not the end of all labor. A relationship with God changes meaningless, wearisome toil into spiritual productivity and purpose."[4]

How about you? How do you react when your burden is heavy and you feel lost? The next time you are, think of Merl laying on his back with a 50 percent chance of a heart attack and a catheter moving along his coronary artery. Merl was at peace; he knew God was by his side with a plan for his life. Merl gave his burden away. So can you.

Merl's story also reveals how God frequently reveals Himself to those of humble background. God often works among the fringes of society, not among the church authorities and leaders. Should Merl's testimony be less believable because he's not an articulate theologian? Why would God reveal Himself to a "hard-drinking reprobate," as Merl describes himself half-jokingly, someone with a wild past and tattoos everywhere? The Bible makes it clear that Jesus was often unimpressed and critical of those at the top of the religious hierarchy. He attacked these church leaders for their hypocrisy, their lack of mercy and compassion, and their pride. He traveled among prostitutes, women, and poor people. His disciples were fishermen and tax collectors. As we discussed in the last chapter, the poorest, most humble people are often the ones who are the richest in spirit.

When I visit Cambodia on medical mission projects, I

encounter people who are on fire with the love of Christ. I see poor, grassroots preachers whose faith is inspiring compared to the relatively lukewarm passion of some affluent, comfortable American church leaders and their congregations. Jesus most often works with people who have been humbled, who are uncorrupted by their wealth and status, who come to Him in a spirit of dependent humility and need. As it says in James 1:27, "Religion that God our Father accepts as pure and faultless is this: to look after orphans and widows in their distress and to keep oneself from being polluted by the world."

Many people in our society who have been blessed with affluence and authority are tempted into believing that they no longer need God. Our society values such traits as self-sufficiency and independence, and there is a widespread belief that those who profess a dependence on God are simply too weak and too afraid to take control of their own lives. But the Bible says, "Blessed are the poor in spirit, for theirs is the kingdom of heaven" (Matt. 5:1-3). In a previous chapter, my friend Chuck spoke of how God works wonders in those whose have a special kind of brokenness and who come before God in a spirit of dependent humility. A hard, proud person who does not claim to need God will be more resistant to God's grace. As is says in Luke 16:15, "You are the ones who justify yourselves in the eyes of men, but God knows your hearts. What is highly valued among men is detestable in God's sight." Self-sufficiency is valued by the world, but a dependent humility is what God prefers.

Merl came away from his divine experience with a passion to do God's work. God's plans for you are no less important. God loves each of us equally, separate from our wealth and our position in society.

My last story concerns an anesthesiologist-turned-psychologist named Bob, who I believe has been touched by God. In February 1994 I gave a lecture at Porter Memorial Hospital's auditorium that was advertised for the lay public. An audience of around 200 people attended. Bob attended the lecture and was later moved to write me a personal letter. In this letter he shared two divine experiences he went through. Later, when I interviewed him, he shared a third divine experience. His experiences, like Merl's, have led to spiritual and interpersonal healing.

At the time of my interview with Bob, he was still struggling to find a church that satisfied him, but because of the following story, he'd been inspired to seek a closer relationship with God. He told me that he'd received almost no religious upbringing from his parents. They had both come from Orthodox Jewish families, but they'd both felt that they had experienced enough of it by the time they raised him. Nor does Bob remember ever desiring a religious education while growing up. His wife had been raised Catholic but had lost interest in it and became inactive by the time she was an adult. Here is his account of the first divine experience he had.

> This happened about a year before the Pope's visit to Denver in 1993. The setting was a meeting of the Denver Jung Society, and it ended with a meditative experience in which we were to imagine being in a safe and comfortable place. The accompanying music was delightful, and I imagined myself being in a gorgeous meadow. Then we were told that something uncertain was happening, and the accompanying music became unsettling. I felt that I was in deep space, but comfortable, not cold and not missing the air. I then imagined that we were on a path in

which we would discover our true path walking to meet us. I was surprised to meet not one person but five. The first was a friend who I had flown with, who I'd experienced a lot of fun with, but who ultimately turned out to be a major pain in my side and my wife's side—a real party boy. This brought us a lot of discomfort and financial trouble and really complicated our lives. It's fair to say that we thoroughly hated him. But when I met him on the path I embraced him and took him into my heart. The next person was a guy that I had gone to graduate school with and butted heads with. On the path I embraced him and took him into my heart. The third person was my younger son. He had been too much like me. He had been troublesome and hyperactive since the day he was born, like me. At that time he'd caused me a lot of discomfort, and I'd been afraid about how he'd handle himself in the world. At the time he was seven or eight years old, and on the path I picked him up and gave him a big hug and took him into my heart. The fourth person was my father, and we sort of hugged at arm's length, if you can call that hugging, because we were never very close; he was kind of a distant guy, but I took him into my heart. The fifth person was Jesus, and we just stood there, heart to heart, and there was absolutely a torrent of energy flowing between us. He looked to me just like He did in the pictures. And that was the end of the experience. Afterwards I thought, "What was Christ doing showing up for me?" I didn't know anything about Him; as far as I knew He was just a nice Jewish boy who went wrong. I didn't know anything about Jesus. I'd been taught that Christians were dangerous. Maybe that's why He showed up. Up until then I didn't have any experience with Him.[5]

A year later Bob had another divine experience. Here it is:

It happened during the Pope's visit to Denver in the summer of 1993. I remember that I was drawn to watch the Pope, and that surprised me because I was from a Jewish background and not really enthusiastic about the Pope's policies or the whole way the Catholic Church conducted itself for the last 1500 years. All I knew was that there was a quality about him I found very attractive. And that quality to me seemed to be of a man who was in constant communication with God. I found that very attractive because I was at the time acutely aware of my separation from God, as well as a separation with individual people, like my mother and many others in my immediate circle. I also felt separated from big chunks of humanity in general; I just felt alienated. The Pope's communication with God seemed like food to me; it felt like something that I was starving for. I remember, on the Saturday before the Pope conducted his Sunday mass, that I asked the Holy Spirit for help. "Help me with all this separation," I prayed. During the mass, I remember there was a Spanish choir singing, and they were singing sweetly; and I couldn't understand their words, but maybe that was good that I couldn't. I just got the sense of the words. They were just swaying back and forth, and it was all so lovely.

Then the camera switched to a couple of guys with beer-bellies hanging out. They looked like frat-boys—not very attractive. They looked like they hadn't shaved since the Pope's visit. They were holding a banner between them that said "God is love" and I thought, "Yeah, yeah, I do believe God is love." And that's when I felt the presence of God enter the family room where I was watching the TV, and it just filled the whole room with His presence. I also noticed that it was filling my son's body. I could just see this divine glow coming from him, even though he's been my most problematic child. And that was it.

The mass was over, and I went by myself to my room and tried to figure out what had just happened. So I was in my room alone, and then I felt the presence of God enter again. There was nothing I could see or anything, but I knew what it was. This time His presence felt so intense that I thought I would surely die, yet die willingly. I thought that I'd be vaporized on the spot. There was no questioning it or resisting it; it was just too big. I did feel that something was burned away, maybe my ego. I can't come up with a good comparison of this experience, except that maybe it was like standing too close to the sun; it was just like being consumed. The night before this experience I had prayed to God for help, since I felt separated from Him. Maybe next time I'll pray for something safer, like a Mercedes!

For the next week I just felt like heaven on Earth. The separation that I had felt was gone, and I felt enveloped with this presence of love. That week when I would drive down East Colfax and look at some of the street people, instead of my usual judgment of "sleazebag" or "dirtball," all I could see was "brother" or "sister." I'll never forget that week. Afterwards I wondered what I should do with my experience, and how [should] I honor it? God's a pretty tough act to follow, and I'll probably be wondering about that question the rest of my life. But I'm so grateful for that experience. It showed me what's possible.[6]

Bob's experiences remind us that Jesus seeks out people regardless of their religious background. Many skeptics point out that people without Christian upbringings shouldn't be judged regarding their relationship with Christ, since they have received no exposure to it. Yet in this instance Jesus appeared to a man who had rarely ever thought about the Man, except as an example of a misguided Jew. Bob's divine experience seems legitimate when examining its themes. During the first experience Bob felt compelled to forgive and make peace with some of the most difficult but important relationships he'd had. Similarly, in the second experience God made His presence known through the figure of Bob's most difficult child, and in the week that followed, after the "burning away of his ego," Bob was able to look upon complete strangers as his brothers and sisters withholding the cynical and superior attitudes he'd sometimes had before. Like Jesus, he was able to see the prostitutes on Colfax as people worthy of love, as opposed to figures worthy of contempt. Though Bob has not yet found a satisfactory place to worship, his divine experiences have led him to seek God.

These experiences are not rare and can happen among large populations. In the last 20 to 30 years in the Middle East, divine visions and dreams, often involving Jesus, have occurred so frequently that an unprecedented number of Muslims have converted to Christianity. The following data comes from Joel Rosenberg, a New York Times best-selling author who lived in the Middle East for several years and interviewed over 150 Christian leaders while writing his book *Inside the Revolution*.[7]

According to Rosenberg, in 1979 there were only about 500 known Muslim converts to Jesus in Iran. "By 2000, a survey of Christian demographic trends reported that there were 220,000 Christians inside Iran, of which between 4000 and 20,000 were Muslim converts. And according to Christian leaders I interviewed for this book, the number of Christ-followers inside their country shot dramatically higher between 2000 and 2008."[8]

Naturally, it can be risky to publicly admit to being a Christian in Iran, so it's hard to guess how many Christians there really are. Rosenberg writes, "An Iranian who directs one of the largest ministries of evangelism and discipleship to Shia Muslims in his country—and is one of the most trusted Iranian ministry leaders in the world—tells me he believes the real number is closer to 7 million believers, or roughly one out of every ten people in Iran."[9]

Lazarus Yegnazar, an Iranian-born evangelist, told Rosenberg, "In the last 20 years, more Iranians have come to Christ than in the last 14 centuries."[10] But most of these new Christians have not been converted by films, ministries, or evangelism. According to Rosenberg, "What is bringing these Iranians to Christ are dreams and visions of Jesus."[11]

Among many other such stories in his book, here is a story Rosenberg heard that was apparently widespread:

> Two Christians [were] driving down the mountains of Iran with a car full of Bibles. Suddenly, their steering wheel jammed and they had to slam on the brakes to keep from driving off the side of the road.

When they looked up, they saw an old man knocking on their windows and asking if they had the books.

"What books?" they asked.

"The books about Jesus," the old man replied. He went on to explain that an angel recently came to him in a vision and told him about Jesus. Later he found out that everyone in the mountain village had had the same vision. They were all brand-new followers of Jesus, but they did not know what to do next. Then the old man had a dream in which Jesus told them to go down the mountain and wait by the road for someone to bring books that would explain how to be a Christian. He obeyed, and suddenly two men with a car full of Bibles had come to a stop right in front of him.[12]

Everyone in the village had had the same vision! Another story involves a Muslim woman who had a dream in which God told her:

"Whatever the two women you are going to meet tomorrow tell you, listen to them." Startled, she went through the next day curious who she would meet. She had no plans to meet anyone, but sure enough, at one point two Iranian Christian women came up to her and explained the message of salvation to her. She obeyed the Lord's directive from the dream, listened carefully, and then bowed her head and prayed to receive Christ as her Savior.[13]

Such stories need not be dismissed as attention-grabbing behavior from desperate people. The Bible speaks often of such divine experiences, as in Joel 2:28: "I will pour out my Spirit on all people. Your sons and daughters will prophesy, your old men will dream dreams, your young men will see visions."

Many of these young people had a *direct conversion experience*; their dreams and visions led directly to them developing a faith in Christ, without needing to go to church first. These experiences remind me of what Paul went through on the road to Damascus, as chronicled in Acts 9.

It is important to note that we should be cautious when someone shares what they believe is a divine experience with us. Doug Groothuis, a Christian theologian, has written a book called *Deceived by the Light*, in which he explains his view, shared by many theologians, that Satan also appears in visions in order to tempt us and lead us astray. This echoes the belief of Maurice Rawlings from the chapter on death and dying, where he reveals the questionable messages that patients receive sometimes by the "light" they witness during a near-death experience. As Groothuis points us, the Bible tells us "the devil and other fallen angels can masquerade as servants of righteousness."[14] In 2 Corinthians 11:3-4 Paul writes, "But I am afraid that just as Eve was deceived by the serpent's cunning, your minds may somehow be led astray from your sincere and pure devotion to Christ. For if someone comes to you and preaches a Jesus other than the Jesus we preached, or if you receive a different spirit from the one you received, or a different gospel from the one you accepted, you put up with it easily enough."

Furthermore, the Bible makes it clear that servants of the devil can also perform miraculous acts. In Revelation 16, demons try to recruit men to fight against God. These demons recruit men by showing them miraculous signs. The Bible teaches that demons have always studied men so that they could more easily mimic them and deceive them. The Book of Deuteronomy suggests that there is a reason why

Jesus allows us to see false visions: "The LORD your God is testing you to find out whether you love him with all your heart and with all your soul" (Deut. 13:3).

How, then, does one distinguish between the visions of God and Satan? One should examine the message of the vision. Doug makes it clear that a vision from God will always be consistent with the Bible's teachings. As I mentioned before, I do not believe divine experiences are common. People may hallucinate, invent visions, or be deceived by a vision sent by Satan. Nevertheless, the Bible makes it clear that God does reveal Himself to people by appearing Himself, sending angels, or performing miraculous signs. These divine experiences transform lives. God wants to inspire us, comfort us, and renew our hope and faith during the crises of our lives; divine experiences are just one of His many tools.

PART 4

THE CARING PROFESSION

CHAPTER 7

FAITH IN SOCIETY:
THE CONFLICT BETWEEN
THE PRIDE OF LEARNING
AND DEPENDENT
HUMILITY BEFORE GOD

The thing that we in medicine must never forget is that we are only the finely tuned instruments on which God plays out his immortal symphony.

—TONI R. YOUNG-HUBER, RN[1]

THE VAST MAJORITY of patients believe in God, believe in the power of prayer, and want their spiritual needs to be met when they are having medical problems. Furthermore, a wide variety of scientific experiments have demonstrated that prayer has striking health benefits, and that religiosity results in greater happiness, stronger marriages, and better health. To a large extent, those spiritual needs are not being met in our hospitals and doctors' offices. In general, the best-educated members of the medical and scientific community have much less of a faith in God than the patients they serve.

Religious teachings also influence their daily conduct to a much lesser extent. Why is this? One reason is the nature of higher education. The higher a student progresses in his or her medical or scientific education, the more religion is ignored or attacked. Another reason is the influence of Darwinism and Freud in scientific and psychiatric education. Another reason is pride. I believe that when education increases without the presence of a guiding moral framework, such as the moral code of the Bible, students often become increasingly self-reliant and even arrogant. God is the author of science and the author of everything good, and He uses these medical and scientific people as part of His plan. And while the benefits of prayer and faith are too mysterious to be fully quantified by scientific experiments, there are still encouraging studies that support what people of faith already know—that prayer and faith make a profound difference in our lives and that caregivers do patients a disservice when they ignore these aspects of our lives.

According to a Gallup poll from 2005, 94 percent of Americans believe in God or a "Universal Spirit,"[2] which is the same figure as the Gallup polls from 1976 revealed.[3] Over the last 50 years, belief in God has hovered around the mid-ninetieth percentile.[4] Polls have shown that the numbers of Americans who believe in life after death are also high, and generally increasing. Today, 80 percent of Americans believe in life after death,[5] compared to 67 percent in 1982.[6]

The belief in God among doctors isn't nearly as high. I did my own survey on various health care professionals in 1993 and found that only 66 percent of physicians believed in God.[7] That number matches the findings of Dr. Maurice Rawlings in his book *Beyond Death's Door.*[8] He reports that 66 percent of physicians answered yes to the questions "Is there a God?" and "Do you believe in an afterlife?" A survey published in the *Journal of Family Practice* found that only 64 percent of doctors claimed to have a belief in God.[9]

Is there something about medical school that drives people away from a belief in God? A friend and former student of mine, Dr. Caroline Sorenson, MD, surveyed her freshmen medical school class of the University of Colorado Health Sciences Center to gauge religious beliefs before their training.[10]

	Yes	No	No Comment
Belief in God	69%	25%	6%
Belief in Life After Death	58%	35%	7%

These numbers suggest that first-year medical students, when it comes to a belief in God, share the same beliefs as seasoned physicians. Among nurses, however, these religious beliefs are dramatically higher. Since 1993 I've delivered many lectures to physicians, nurses, and other health care workers. I've surveyed these audiences many times and have found that 95 percent of nurses consistently claimed to believe in both the existence of God and in an afterlife.

Let's examine the effects education has on religious beliefs. The University of Chicago surveyed thousands of people on a variety of religious questions, breaking them into categorizes based on the amount of education they had completed.[11] To summarize, the average person was three times as likely as someone with an advanced degree to say, "We trust too much in science and not enough in religion." Almost three times as many people with an advanced degree "definitely did not believe in heaven," compared with the average person. The numbers weren't as dramatic when it came to following one's own conscience, but people with an advanced degree were more likely to value their own consciences over the teachings of their church or synagogue.

We also found significant differences in belief between psychiatrists and their patients. One survey found that 95 percent of psychiatric patients, compared to only 43 percent of psychiatrists, believe in God or a Universal Spirit.[12] A survey conducted by the American Psychiatric Association found that about half the psychiatrists surveyed considered themselves agnostics or atheists, whereas only 1 to 5 percent of the general population considered themselves agnostics or atheists. More than half of the psychiatrists surveyed said they attended church "rarely" or "never."[13]

Similar results have been found in other surveys of psychiatrists. By a ratio of well over two to one, patients have more of a belief in God than their psychiatrists. What could account for this wide discrepancy? Certainly the influence of Sigmund Freud is a factor. Freud is considered the father of modern psychiatry. He was outspoken in his belief that religious teachings are "illusions, fulfillments of the oldest, strongest and most urgent wishes of mankind."[14] He claimed that religious belief is a "universal obsessional neurosis."[15] One of Freud's influential followers, the psychologist Albert Ellis, wrote that religiosity "is significantly correlated with emotional disturbance" and that "the less religious (people) are, the more emotionally healthy they will tend to be."[16]

Despite Freud's influence, many of his fundamental teachings have been hotly contested and refuted in many circles within the last 50 years. Psychoanalysis, which he founded, is widely considered a "pseudo-science"[17] and is elsewhere considered the "the most stupendous confidence trick of the twentieth century."[18] According to Kevin MacDonald, who writes for *Skeptic* magazine, many of Freud's key concepts have lost so much favor among academics that they are no longer taught. He writes, "Now 100 years after its inception, the theories of the Oedipal complex, childhood sexuality, and the sexual etiology of the neuroses remain without any independent empirical validation and play no role whatever in mainstream developmental psychology."[19] Time has not strengthened Freud's claims that religion is a form of neurosis or an illusion. As we will demonstrate later, much empirical evidence shows that religiosity, faith, and a committed prayer life are beneficial to a person's long-term physical and mental health.

Since psychiatry began, the issue of religion and spirituality has often been ignored or mentioned primarily as a sign of mental disorder. Consider what the International Review of Psychiatry offers on the subject:

> More often than being frankly hostile to religion, psychiatrists have simply ignored it. Standard textbooks of psychiatry pay scant attention to this aspect of human life. They do not mention religion as a factor in personality development or identity, much less as a potential source of support for a healthy personality or sustenance during times of illness or trouble. Where religion is mentioned, it is pathologized.[20]

Regarding the beliefs of scientists in general, here is a report from a telephone survey in 2009 of the world's largest general scientific society, the American Association for the Advancement of Science (AAAS): only 33 percent believed in God.[21] As with the case of psychiatrists, this is much lower than the rate of the general population.

Why is it that people with more advanced degrees, particularly those studying science and medicine, like physicians, psychiatrists, and scientists, display such a significant lack of faith in religion? One of the reasons is that Darwinism dominates scientific education. There isn't even much of a debate; most teachers act as if the debate has been settled, and Darwin is triumphant. The theory of evolution is treated as the *fact* of evolution. Many of the key stories from the Bible are treated like fairy tales that reasonable adults should be eager to dispense with.

Darwinists shouldn't be so confident. There are still major question marks about the way evolution works, and plenty of scientists and physicians believe that the evidence supports the idea of an Intelligent Designer. I will not present an exhaustive discussion of evolution, but I will share a single argument that Darwinists have not been able to refute. It comes from Lee Strobel's book *The Case for a Creator*.

> Let's consider just how complex life is. The capacity of DNA to store information vastly exceeds that of any other known system; it is so efficient that all information needed to specify an organism as complex as man weighs less than a few thousand millionths of a gram. Furthermore, DNA does not simply contain a lot of information. Nearly all that information must be present for that cell to live and function properly. Living cells deactivate immediately if only a small component is deactivated or removed. The probability of life originating from an accident is comparable to the probability of the unabridged dictionary resulting from an explosion in a printing shop.[22]

> How could a random mix of elements have been so precise and complex? Is it credible that random processes could have constructed a reality, the smallest element of which—a functional protein or

gene—is complex beyond our own creative capacities, a reality which is the very antithesis of chance, which excels in every sense anything produced by the intelligence of man?[23]

How can lifeless dust acquire the miraculous ability to have self-awareness, to suddenly develop senses with which to perceive the universe, to suddenly develop the motivation to reproduce? In what way does dust intrinsically contain the need to evolve? The only way to explain the complexity of life is to bring in an external, purposeful, creative and organizing force to impose order. Without a Creator, it's not possible.[24]

I believe that science is a gift from God. Through science God's existence and His glory are revealed. Contrary to the opinions of many godless scientists, science and faith are not antagonistic. The more I study science, the more my faith is strengthened. Furthermore, as Ralph Waldo Emerson said, "All I have seen teaches me to trust the Creator for all I have not seen."[25] When I look back on my undergraduate medical training, I feel misled by some of my instruction, and it doesn't surprise me that so many students of science become skeptical about God.

Let's discuss another reason why so many of those with advanced degrees try to live their lives without God: pride and the attractions of self-sufficiency. I do believe there is a natural temptation among those with advanced degrees to feel self-sufficient because of their abilities. The more the Bible is removed from the center of our moral education, the more we are convinced that we don't need God, that we can construct our own rules and morality, that science has given us the power to be self-sufficient. I believe this attitude ignores the limitations of science and pulls us away from God's plan for our lives.

I believe America's secular school system, especially in higher education, equips people with the knowledge—and therefore the power—to achieve what they desire. However, it offers them little in the way of lasting wisdom. I believe that when power increases without the development of a guiding moral framework, that power often corrupts a person's humility and morals. Many people use the words *knowledge* and *wisdom* interchangeably, but there is a difference. I believe knowledge is simply the acquisition of facts, theories, and experiences. Wisdom is the ability to take that knowledge and make moral decisions based on lasting principles and truths. Much of this wisdom, I contend, can be found in the Bible.

In 1864, during the Civil War, Abraham Lincoln was given a Bible by a group of black abolitionists to thank him for his struggle to free the slaves. Lincoln made the following comments about the Bible.

> In regard to this great book, I have but to say it is the best gift God has given to man. All the good Savior gave to the world was communicated through this book. But for it we could not know right from wrong. All things most desirable for man's welfare, here and hereafter, are to be found portrayed in it.[26]

Indeed, the Bible has been the dominant moral guide for the Western world. To what do godless people owe their allegiance? In most cases, to themselves. If there is no divine judgment and no absolute morality, then most people turn to the gratification of their worldly desires through materialism, self-satisfaction, and the acquisition of power. Sinatra celebrated his self-reliance when he sang "My Way," and many people celebrate this as an ideal worth pursuing. If there is no responsibility for our actions aside from the justice imposed by other men, the priority becomes avoiding getting caught. Seeking righteousness for its own sake in a world of men clawing for power becomes a philosophy for the naïve, a strategy for getting left behind in the rat race. "Nice guys finish last," as the cliché says. I am not saying that the best-educated people don't value morality. But there are no Ten Commandments of secular humanism. There is no agreed-upon moral framework among atheists.

For those who do not acknowledge a power higher than themselves, what is there to value? One answer is *themselves*. People honor themselves for their talent, their gifts, their worldly success. In my opinion, it is a philosophy built on sinking sand. It is certainly possible to develop one's gifts, but we are no more responsible for the presence of our gifts in the first place than we are responsible for the creation of the Earth.

Despite what people with advanced degrees claim to believe about God, other studies have suggested that they pray *just as often* as those with less education. A poll at the University of Chicago asked people with varying educational backgrounds, "How often do you pray?"[27]

	Daily or More	Once to Several Times a Week	Less Than Once a Week	Never
Total	55%	22%	22%	2%
Not a HS Graduate	59%	21%	18%	1%
HS Graduate	53%	22%	22%	1%
Bachelor's Degree	53%	21%	24%	2%
Graduate Degree	56%	14%	27%	3%

How surprising that only 66 percent of doctors and only 43 percent of psychiatrists believe in God—versus 95 percent of the general population—and yet just as many people with graduate degrees pray on a daily basis as the general population! Evidently this highly skeptical population still feels a strong desire to pray. Perhaps their inner longing for God overcomes intellectual obstacles. Perhaps the saying "Everybody in a foxhole needs God" extends to this situation. In the face of life's worst calamities, in the face of the humbling and terrifying experiences we all go through, we are all reminded of the puny limitations of our self-reliance. This "special kind of brokenness" reminds us we are only able to convince ourselves that we don't need God when life is exceptionally safe and comfortable.

Should these self-sufficient people, when they are responsible for a patient's health and well-being, be so certain that prayer and religiosity play no role in our health and well-being? Let's examine some of the many experiments coming from a wide variety of health-related topics that refute such a belief. The study of prayer in the laboratory setting is only beginning. The bulk of the studies have taken place in the last 20 years, and while many experiments have been inconclusive, proponents of prayer are gaining plenty of new converts. Even if the scientific community is skeptical in general, the general population has much stronger convictions regarding prayer, and they are eager to see their convictions validated. Larry Dossey, MD, the best-selling author of several books concerning prayer, claims in his book *Healing Words*:

> The most important reason to examine prayer in healing is simply that, at least some of the time, it works. The evidence is simply overwhelming that prayer functions at a distance to change physical processes....These data...are so impressive that I have come to regard them as among the best kept secrets in medical science.[28]

Possibly the most well known study was published in 1988 by Dr. Randolph Byrd, a cardiologist at the University of California San Francisco School of Medicine. Nearly 400 patients in a coronary care unit were randomized into two groups. One group received intercessory prayer from a group outside the hospital; the other was a control group. It was a double-blind study, which means that neither the patients nor the doctors and nurses involved knew which patients were being prayed for. The patients that received intercessory prayer suffered fewer deaths; were less likely to require endotracheal intubation and ventilator support; required fewer potent drugs, such as diuretics and antibiotics; experienced a lower incidence of pulmonary edema (fluid in the lungs); and required cardiopulmonary resuscitation less often. Dr. Byrd's findings galvanized other researchers into expanding his work and earned grudging respect from many skeptics.[29]

In 2001, more striking results were published from a study in Seoul, Korea. In this case, 199 women at an in vitro fertilization clinic were divided into groups. Once again, neither the hospital caregivers nor the patients knew that the study was taking place. This time, Christian prayer groups from around the world prayed that women in one of the groups would become pregnant. They were given pictures of individual women they were supposed to pray for. The women in the "prayed-for" groups became pregnant twice as often, a startling result. Follow-up studies were immediately planned.[30]

This study by Dr. Rogerio Lobo, MD, chair of obstetrics and gynecology at Columbia University School of Medicine, appeared in the September 2001 edition of the *Journal of Reproductive Medicine*:

> Other promising studies have been done regarding the effects of prayer in helping people with blood infections. Between 1990 and 1996, 3300 patients were admitted to a hospital with blood infections. Once again, the group was split into a control group and a group that received intercessory prayer. To determine the effects of prayer, researchers monitored fatality rates, the number of days patients had elevated fevers, and the duration of their stay in the hospital.
>
> Although the fatality rates between the two groups were similar, the group that was prayed for suffered fewer days with fever and spent less time in the hospital.[31]

As encouraging as these results are, it is obvious that scientific studies are not the best way to understand or showcase the power of prayer. Treating prayer as just one more variable in an experiment assumes that we have a good understanding of prayer's mysteries, which seems to me to be a gross overestimation of our knowledge. A chemist boils water confident that he can measure the atomic weights of hydrogen and oxygen; a scientist who studies the effects of prayers among hundreds of individuals he doesn't know should only make the most humble of conclusions. Since determining the power of prayer is so much more subjective than determining the answer to an algebra equation, let us turn to the insights of caregivers who have spent their careers observing the role of prayer in their patients' well-being.

In a previous chapter, Rev. Bud Sparling spoke about how he viewed prayer as an attitudinal posture in which he tried to maintain a constant state of praise and thankfulness toward God. Similarly, many doctors notice that patients with strong prayer lives often develop a constant state of peace and acceptance and that those patients usually enjoy superior health and milder, more peaceful deaths. As recounted in *Healing Words*, Larry Dossey interviewed doctors who dealt with patients who experienced SRCs, or spontaneous regressions of cancer, in which malignant tumors inexplicably shrunk. It has been estimated that such miraculous occurrences happen once in every 100,000 cases. One doctor said, "Often a prayerful, prayer-like attitude of devotion and acceptance—not robust, aggressive prayer for specific outcomes, including eradication of the cancer—precedes the cure."[32] This attitude mirrors the attitude Dr. Don Sweeting spoke of in the last chapter when he was stressing what one's priorities should be during prayer. He said, "That relationship [with God] is the ultimate issue. The ultimate issue is not us getting better... God's healing is not always done in this life."[33]

What about the effects of prayer on people's general health

and sense of well-being over a lifetime? If intercessory prayer can help heal people during times of sickness, shouldn't prayer act as a preventative measure when people are not sick? Should we expect people with strong prayer lives to be happier, healthier people? Dr. Dale Matthews and Dr. Bernie Siegel think so. A study following over 26,000 people over the course of 18 years concluded that religious people were more likely to be happy and employed. The main point of the study was to determine what happened to people who lost their religion. The religiously active people were much likely to say they were "very happy" and also had a much better history of staying employed. These results come from a 1992 study.[34]

Another study cited by Dr. Matthews followed 1650 individuals over 40 years, a period far exceeding that of most studies. The adult respondents were asked about their religious beliefs and practices and asked to rate their overall life satisfaction, including the factors of marriage, work, and community. Respondents who attended church reported a far higher degree of overall life satisfaction, and those who reported strong religious beliefs were much more likely to have happy marriages. Even after researchers applied controls to the data to account for the influences of gender and income, church attendance and personal religious belief were still powerful factors in determining the happiness of these individuals.[35]

Does increased religiosity correspond to better health? Dr. Jeffrey Levin considered many different studies and found that even among less strict denominations there was a "trend towards better health and less morbidity and mortality, across the board, in the presence of higher levels of religiosity."[36] The trend is observed for many aspects of physical and mental health. Dr. Levin reports that there was a significant link between religious involvement and improved health in 75 percent of the studies he examined.[37]

Some of these results can be criticized, but this criticism doesn't explain the results of Dr. Byrd's study or of other studies in which patients didn't know they were receiving prayer. Regardless, I don't expect the scientific studies presented in this chapter to prove how or why or even if prayer works, or that religious people are healthier than nonreligious people. I present these findings as a source of validation for those who already believe in prayer and as a source of hope for those who are skeptical. So far studies have shown significant health gains from prayer. Dr. Matthews mirrors Dr. Levin's assertion that 75 percent of the studies on prayer "have confirmed health benefits."[38]

In the scientific community these results are still controversial. Despite my own conviction in the power of prayer, I don't expect the scientific community to ever "prove" the power of prayer. The mysteries of prayer are beyond the scope of science to pin down and quantify. The scientific method is the observation, identification, description, experimental investigation, and theoretical explanation of phenomena. It is a systematic method of isolating the variables that interact in order to produce these phenomena. The method's reliance on experimentation and the unbiased collection of data have made it a peerless tool in understanding and harnessing the forces and materials in the world around us. But the separation of phenomena into individual components can only be taken seriously when the components are easily understood and defined. As I mentioned before, the atomic weight of a water molecule can be defined and explained, and remains predictable in a variety of situations. But isolating prayer in the same manner assumes an understanding of God's power that no respectable scientist should claim. How can science quantifiably measure such benefits of prayer as peace of mind or the improvement of one's relationship with God?

Consider the example of a patient suffering from hopelessness because of the worsening of his cancer. Imagine that fervent prayer reconnected that patient to God and filled his heart with peace before death. How could an experiment measure that victory? That patient's death would be recorded in an experiment as a failure of prayer to heal. As a result, the awesome victory of the occasion, from God's perspective, of reconnecting with one of His children before his death would be unappreciated by science. I do not mean to discredit science. The quality of my practice is partially founded on the achievements of science. But any good scientist will also recognize the limits of science.

Hopefully, more of the skeptics who influence the medical community will begin to appreciate what the vast majority of patients already know: that God is in charge of life and death and that the many caregivers who view their work as a sacred calling are not willing to deny Him the credit.

It is important to note that for thousands of years the church heavily influenced the philosophy of medicine and the establishment of churches, and that church men and medical workers weren't always so antagonistic. Today's hospitals were mostly founded by churches, and their mission statements are still based on Scripture. These words appear on the cornerstone at the Swedish Hospital in Englewood, Colorado: "To the glory of God and the service of humanity." Furthermore, the vast majority of nurses, who spend more time with patients than other caregivers, also acknowledge God's sovereignty, and their faith influences the way they care for patients. For caregivers like these, science is not opposed to faith; it is a gift from God. Science and faith should work in harmony to provide excellent care. Caregivers should not pretend that science alone has all the answers.

I know the temptations physicians feel to be arrogant about their education and power, since I have wrestled with this struggle as a physician and continue to do so. How do we approach the arrogant, self-reliant unbeliever? Lecturing with a condescending manner only alienates unbelievers and often hardens their hearts against God's plan. I've made this mistake myself. One night, my wife and I attended a dinner party with two of our friends, a physician and his wife. He is an intelligent physician and scientist and a non-Christian. He cares deeply for my wife and I. Before dinner started we began debating on the theory of evolution and other arguments for and against Christianity. We didn't really listen to each other; we aggressively argued our agendas. Dinner ended up being tense and awkward. Fortunately, my wife pointed out the faults in my approach the next day. She made me realize that being unloving, cold, and aggressive is not the way in which God wants us to be His witnesses. Once again, my wife was right. I invited my friend to breakfast, apologized, and asked for his forgiveness. I affirmed my love for him and his wife. A week later, as it happens, I was inserting a stent into a coronary artery of that same friend, who was experiencing chest pain. During the insertion of the stent, he experienced the worst pain of his life. He looked up at me with fear in his eyes. I knew the coronary artery was now open and the flow through the stent was excellent. I told him with a reassuring confidence that he would be all right. I prayed for him silently.

This encounter reminded me that God has called on

His church and His disciples to be like salt and light in the world. We should present our faith in an attractive, flavorful manner. When we witness to an unbeliever, we should share what God has done in our own lives. We should reflect God's love and grace in our lives, and we should express our gratitude and thanks to Him. When we exhibit the peace and joy that comes from His grace, we will naturally draw attention to the merits of our faith. When we act superior, we are misrepresenting our faith. However, I do believe it is sometimes appropriate to challenge nonbelievers, who often, from a spiritual point of view, are standing on sinking sand. When God calls on us to be like salt, a preserver against immorality and untruth, He expects us to proclaim the truth. But we should do it with love in our hearts and great confidence, because ultimately God is in control of transforming people's hearts. As I said before, we are only the instruments on which He plays out His immortal symphony. In Colossians 4:3–6, the Bible speaks of how believers may approach non-believers:

> Pray for us, too, that God may open a door for our message, so that we may proclaim the mystery of Christ…Pray that I may proclaim it clearly, as I should. Be wise in the way you act toward outsiders; make the most of every opportunity. Let your conversation be always full of grace, seasoned with salt, so that you may know how to answer everyone.

We will make no headway with people when their hearts are closed. When we aggressively try to evangelize them in such a situation, we are likely to harden their hearts against us even more. So, we must be watchful for the door to open.

When are people more likely to be open-hearted? As we

spoke of in earlier chapters, when we are poor in spirit, when a "special kind of brokenness" has made us humbler and less self-sufficient, when a catastrophic illness or loss has broken down our layers of security we will be more aware of the limitations of self-reliance and more aware of our dependence on God's grace. We should watch closely for these opportunities to bear witness.

In the midst of His symphony, God wants us to be equipped with the knowledge and skills to aid patients. But any degrees or honors we achieve must be accompanied by humility. As E. M. Bounds says, "The pride of learning is against the dependent humility of prayer."[39] And when dealing with patients who overwhelmingly rely on faith and the power of prayer, we must become instruments that are not insensitive or dismissive of these profoundly powerful tools, for as it says in James 5:16, "The prayer of a righteous man is powerful and effective." With that in mind, let us remember not only to pray on behalf of our patients and loved ones, but also on behalf of their caregivers. Let us pray that their hearts remain open to the lessons of the dying room, open to the spiritual needs of their patients, and open to God's saving grace.

CHAPTER 8

THE CARING and HEALING PROFESSION: OUR ULTIMATE ADVOCATE

A NUMBER OF YEARS ago a 70-year-old male patient came into the emergency room complaining of chest pain. While playing saxophone with some friends at a club, a sudden pain lanced through his chest. Afterwards he felt out of breath. His wife drove him to the ER that night. A few tests were taken, which ended up being negative, at which point the ER doctors reassured him and sent him home. His wife, however, had a hunch that her husband's condition was not quite as harmless as they were led to believe. She called my office and discussed her hunch with my nurse practitioner, Barb Van Horne. The wife let Barb know in no uncertain terms that something was wrong with her husband. Barb listened to the story and sent him back to the hospital, insistent that someone was going to take another look. I was called in to see him in the morning, and after a preliminary investigation I said that I was unsure about the problem. I ordered an echocardiogram (sound wave test) and other diagnostic tests to get more information.

At around four o'clock in the afternoon my day was winding down. I had a dinner reservation for that evening with my friend, Dr. Brack Hattler, a heart surgeon I frequently worked with. I read the echocardiogram and was shocked to learn that the patient's diagnosis was an acute aortic dissection, which means the main artery carrying blood from the heart had ripped. I immediately paged Dr. Hattler and told him that dinner was cancelled and that I needed him to operate on my patient right away. Dr. Hattler dropped what he was doing and immediately rushed to the operating room. As he and the operating team were opening up the patient's chest, the patient's aorta ruptured on the table. If this had happened anywhere but on the operating table, the patient would have quickly died. The aorta is the largest blood vessel in the body, and if the surgeon hadn't been there to close off the wound with his hand, the patient would have quickly spilled out his entire blood supply. Luckily, the patient was hooked up to the heart and lung machine, which effectively circulated and oxygenated his blood for him. Ice-cold water was poured over his heart, which stopped it from beating, and a graft was inserted in the aorta, which effectively healed the rupture. He was later sent home, where he made a full recovery. Had it not been for the stubborn advocacy of his wife, who wouldn't let the results of a few tests overcome her gut instinct, her husband would certainly have died at home.

Barb told me that wives frequently drag their husbands in for more tests and more care. The husbands, macho at all ages, are often uncomfortable asking for help. Barb has worked in cardiac care for over 30 years. The symptoms of heart disease are often subtle; a minor ache, a pain in the chest that comes and goes. Without the pestering of wives, a lot of tough guys wouldn't be here anymore. Had we relied purely on my patient's preliminary lab results, we wouldn't have had a reason to keep looking for answers. Had my nurse practitioner not listened and taken on the responsibility, the patient would not have received the test that determined the correct diagnosis. In this case the patient's wife, Barb, and Dr. Hattler functioned as the patient's advocates.

What was going on here? Was the patient's recovery simply a result of caregiver initiative? Was it merely luck? Who ultimately controls the power of life and death? Once again, I'm convinced that God is the ultimate patient advocate. We caregivers should be reminded of the Bible's lessons in 1 Corinthians 1:31, "Let him who boast, boast in the Lord." This patient's recovery, like so many others, re-inspired me to say, "Praise the Lord."

This chapter will examine the caring profession, which encompasses all of the workers whose job it is to care for the physical, emotional, and spiritual needs of patients. We will also discuss the characteristics of excellent patient care and also what factors contribute to inadequate care and diagnostic errors. We will examine the roles of patient advocates. We will focus in on the nursing profession, since nurses provide such constant patient advocacy, and also examine the challenges confronting administrators in an age when the growing pressures to seek profit can compromise quality care.

Who are patient advocates? A patient advocate is anyone who looks out for the well-being of a patient and acts in accordance with the patient's interests, encouraging him, defending him, and helping him secure the best possible care. A patient advocate may act as a spokesperson for the patient, explaining his or her needs and concerns to caregivers or demanding action when those needs aren't met. These advocates are key figures in the caring profession.

The word *caring* does not simply mean to be concerned or interested in someone else's well-being. Caring implies that a burden is being taken on, that a responsibility has been accepted. This burden does not end on a predictable schedule;

it is one reason why doctors do not work 9-to-5 jobs. They should not go home until the essential work is done. As one hospital administrator told me, caring for patients is "not like selling shoes. It's so much more than that. It's a sacred calling." Cutting corners and rushing through patient questions dishonors this calling. I spoke to a number of nurses, administrators, and physician assistants, and nearly all of them repeated this idea that their work is a privilege and a sacred calling.

The most obvious members of the caring profession include those involved in direct patient care: the doctors, nurses, nursing assistants, physician assistants, and medical technicians. Few people realize how many others provide care. There are the administrators, paramedics, and hospital chaplains. There are the support professionals from churches, including pastors, caring ministries, and members of prayer chains. There are the staff members at hospices, nursing homes, and orphanages. There are the receptionists, who often bear the brunt of patients' anger and frustration. There are also those who may not provide direct care but who help provide a safe, efficient, clean environment, like the janitors, engineers, painters, and so many more. We should not take their service for granted.

I have traveled many times to Cambodia with the Christian Medical Ministry to Cambodia/Jeremiah's Hope to survey and assist their relatively primitive health care system. While there our team found an old, decrepit clinic, which we renovated to the point that it met Western standards. I still have the vivid memory of one of our first successful surgical procedures in the new clinic. We felt quite pleased with the procedure's outcome. The next day, upon returning to the clinic, we saw street children playing in the used, bloody surgical refuse from the previous day. Our team had assumed that the refuse would be discarded in a safe manner. This episode reminded us how we'd often taken for granted essential work like garbage removal, and we felt humbled.

The many members of the caring profession function like the various cells in the human body. All are important and interdependent. The brain cells are dependent on the circulatory system for nourishment. Doctors are often viewed as the heroes of the caring profession. In many cases, doctors spend only 5 to 10 minutes a day with their patients. The nurses, by contrast, often spend 8 to 10 hours around the patient, doing many of the most mundane, unpleasant, but necessary work. As we will discuss later, they are usually the patient's most consistent advocates. When certain professions within the caring profession act superior to other professions, they are ignoring the fact that they play only one role among the hundreds of roles needed to provide quality care.

As we examine the art of caring for patients, I am reminded of my first days as a medical student when I was reading the introduction to "The Approach of the Patient" in Harvey's *The Principles and Practice of Medicine*.[1] In Harvey's text, I came across a passage by Dr. Francis Weld Peabody. I will repeat the essence of the passage because it is rightfully considered a classic essay on the care of the patient.

> The practice of medicine in its broadest sense includes the whole relationship of the physician with his patient. It is an art, based to an increasing extent on the medical sciences but comprising much that still remains outside the realm of any science. The art of medicine and the science of medicine are not antagonistic but supplementary to each other. There is no more contradiction between the science of medicine

and the art of medicine than between the science of aeronautics and the art of flying. Good practice presupposes an understanding of the sciences that contributes to the structure of modern medicine, but it is obvious that sound professional training should include a much broader equipment.

The treatment of disease may be entirely impersonal; the care of a patient must be completely personal. The significance of the intimate personal relationship between physician and patient cannot be too strongly emphasized, for in an extraordinarily large number of cases both diagnosis and treatment are directly dependent on it, and failure of the young physician to establish this relationship accounts for much of his ineffectiveness in the care of patients.

What is spoken of as a "clinical picture" is not just a photograph of a man sick in bed; it is an impressionistic painting of the patient surrounded by his home, his work, his relations, his friends, his joys, sorrows, hopes, and fears.

Thus, the physician who attempts to take care of a patient while he neglects those factors which contribute to the emotional life of this patient is as unscientific as the investigator who neglects to control all the conditions which may affect his experiment. The good physician knows his patients through and through and his knowledge is bought dearly. Time, sympathy, and understanding must be lavishly dispensed but the reward is to be found in that personal bond which forms the greatest satisfaction of the practice of medicine. One of the essential qualities of the clinician is interest in humanity, *for the secret of the care of the patient is in caring for the patient.*[2] [emphasis added]

These ideas inspired me at an early stage of my career. Dr. Peabody's life and his teachings are worth exploring briefly. He was born in 1881, eventually attended Harvard Medical School and became physician-in-chief of the Fourth Medical Service at the Boston City Hospital. In 1926 he lectured from his essay "The Care of the Patient," and four years later his writings on the subject were gathered in a book entitled *Doctor and Patient*.[3]

At the turn of the century, scientific advances were making medicine more effective but also vastly more complex, and medical schools were spending so much time cramming students with scientific knowledge that they didn't adequately train them in the art of establishing a trusting relationship with patients. Dr. Peabody wrote:

> To begin with, the fact must be accepted that one cannot expect to become a skillful practitioner of medicine in the four or five years allotted to the medical curriculum. Medicine is not a trade to be learned but a profession to be entered. It is an ever-widening field that requires continued study and prolonged experience in close contact with the sick.[4]

In today's medical environment, there are increasing pressures placed on caregivers to increase their turnover rate. One of Dr. Peabody's fundamental points is that excellent medical care takes time. When caregivers hastily value turnover rates over excellent care, the results are often rushed diagnoses and the lack of an intimate, trusting relationship with their patients. It leads to the more frequent complaint from patients that doctors treat them not as individuals with complex psychological needs, but as illnesses without personalities. The results may be an overreliance on laboratory tests and less of the more subtle analysis that comes from speaking with and observing patients and sharing insights with fellow caregivers. For example, some macho patients may be unwilling to admit serious pains. Others may want to hide smoking habits. Others may believe that their situation is much more hopeless than it really is as a result of misinterpreting information or receiving bad information.

Dr. Peabody, ironically, presented his lectures at a time in his life when he knew he was dying of stomach cancer. He had complained numerous times to his own doctors about weight loss, pain, and nausea, but because his X-rays and lab results revealed no problems, his condition was misdiagnosed repeatedly over several years. The man who condemned the contemporary over-reliance on scientific tests ended up dying because his own lab results were given emphasis over his own testimony.[5]

When reviewing the medical literature, the following five factors contribute consistently to diagnostic errors by physicians in clinical medicine. These factors include:

1. Not obtaining a reliable history and physical examination of the patient and not accounting for abnormal symptoms, signs or laboratory results that aren't consistent with the clinical impression

2. Not obtaining routine screening tests or other appropriate procedures

3. Not realizing that X-ray or imaging studies may not disclose pathological changes

4. The failure to recognize new illnesses developing in the presence of previously diagnosed chronic disease

5. Not reviewing periodically the records of patients with prolonged illnesses and/or repeating physical examinations[6]

As I wrote in this paper:

The solution to the problem of diagnostic errors in clinical practice is a continuous one for all physicians. On the subject of diagnostic errors, Francis Carter Wood, MD, commented in 1919:

> "...the only way to improve diagnosis is to follow our cases with the greatest of care and to study our practical results and those of others. Failures in diagnosis are often due, not so much to lack of knowledge, as to lack of thoroughness and care in examination. Too much reliance is placed on laboratory reports, which are popularly supposed to have an infallibility with which no laboratory man would credit them. One way in which to improve the treatment of patients is to have students in the hospital wards. In teaching them, the physician teaches himself."

As physicians we must always remain students. Dr. William Osler commented that educators should strive to "give him/her good methods and a proper point of view, and all other things will be added as their experience grows."[7]

One of my mentors from the Baylor College of Medicine, Dr. David Y. Graham, stressed the importance of medical caregivers being able to say "I don't know" when dealing with the challenges of individual cases. Doctors, as I've mentioned before, tend to be unusually confident, even arrogant, about their abilities. They become accustomed to excelling on their exams and handling their challenges with a rare, quick-thinking decisiveness. It leaves them less humble than they should be about the mysteries of the healing process. Many times patients have come in to my office complaining of atypical chest pains that aren't easily explained by our standard procedures. I've frequently seen doctors conclude that the patient had nothing to worry about. In many cases, those chest pains end up being symptoms of life-threatening conditions. In such cases, I'll often say, "I don't understand yet," when analyzing such a case. When I do, I am letting the patient know that the search for answers goes on, that I am not closing the door on their case, that my burden for them remains. By comparison, if one of my colleagues or I rush through the care of the patient, tells them too quickly what their diagnosis is, and tells them not to worry, we may be shirking our responsibilities in order to lighten our loads. We've ended the sacred process of figuring out the best possible solution. In those cases, our diagnoses had better be right!

Many times I have decided on the correct diagnosis only after discovering a small piece of additional patient history that could have been easily overlooked. Questioning nurses is one of the best ways to pick up new clues about a patient's condition. Nurses spend much more time around patients than physicians. Furthermore, they are often warmer and less intimidating than physicians in their patient interaction.

As a result, patients often confide in them more often than with their doctors.

Nevertheless, when I talked to nurses who had been working for several decades, they told me that most times doctors won't let nurses critique them. Mary Soltau, a registered nurse in my office, started nursing in the late seventies. She told me that for most of her career there was an unspoken rule between doctors and nurses: the nurses were not supposed to point out physician mistakes. On several occasions, when Mary noticed doctors misinterpreting vital signs or not pursuing a patient's complaints, the doctors denied that they had made mistakes. Because nurses spend so much more time around patients, they notice things doctors miss. Unless a doctor allows his diagnostic conclusions to be critiqued on occasion by his nurses, he is doing a disservice to his patients. In my office, it is assumed that I'm not 100 percent right. I encourage my staff to speak up when they believe that I'm missing something. I can't let my pride interfere in the care of the patient.

I talked to several hospital administrators about nurses. Ruthita Fike is the CEO of Loma Linda Medical Center Hospital System in California. She was previously the executive vice president of Centura Health, the largest health care provider in the state of Colorado. She told me that there is currently a nursing crisis in this country. Nurses from all generations confirm that too many in their profession are overworked, lack a sense of teamwork, and are too burdened with busywork to give direct patient care, which most often is what inspires them and got them into the profession in the first place. Paperwork alone takes away from much direct care. As Ruthita points out, "We've discovered our systems are so complex that nurses are only able to spend 10 to 15 minutes out of an hour dealing directly with the patients."[8]

Mary Essary, who has been a nurse for almost 40 years, told me that nurses simply can't do what they're being asked to do today:

> Some of their bosses seem to think, "Let's not even care how much they're already doing. Let's just keep dumping on the work." There's no doubt in my mind nursing has changed for the worse. It scares me to death for the patients.[9]

Both Mary Soltau and Mary Essary speak of their early days of work in nonprofit health care as if it were a golden age of nursing. Before the rise of for-profit hospitals, Mary Soltau says it was standard procedure for hospital nurses to give patients massages, brush their dentures, and get them to bed properly.[10] As time passed, nurses have been replaced by nurses' aids with less experience and training, and the quality of care has suffered. Today, there are many more traveling or "floating" nurses working. By "floating" nurses I mean nurses who do not become permanent staff members of a particular hospital or clinic but who float from job to job to fill vacancies or provide temporary help. Because nurses used to stay at their jobs longer, they developed the cohesion and familiarity and efficiency so essential for quality care. When I talk to younger nurses, I am somewhat disheartened by how many dislike their jobs and feel too exhausted at the end of the day to make up for the rewarding aspects of direct care.

Nurses are taught during training that they will not have to care for more than four patients at a time. My daughter Laurie, who previously was a cardiac telemetry nurse, said that she has had to care for more than six patients at a time. In California, there is a law against overextending care like this. In Colorado, where many hospitals have operated for years despite unfilled nursing positions, overextension is just a part of the territory. Linda Scheurer, RN, ANP, who has worked for over 25 years as a nurse practitioner, says that many nurses today are expected to do certain tasks twice as fast as they used to.[11]

Mary Essary pointed out other reasons why nurses are having trouble. Some nurses enter the health care field for the wrong reasons. Because there are always nursing shortages these days, nursing is almost a guaranteed job. This attracts many people who just aren't prepared to work as hard as the job demands; their sights are too much on the guaranteed paycheck. She told me, "Nursing used to be about the art of caring and service, and of course it also meant lots of hard work. I doubt whether that's always being taught today."[12]

Mary Essary also believes there is less teamwork today among nurses. "If I ever thought I would be in this profession all by myself, I wouldn't be in it."[13] Today, nursing teams are frequently broken up. The modern age makes it easier for people to be mobile. And, as health care has become more diversified, there are wider differences in reimbursements, benefits, and working conditions. Naturally, many nurses follow where the best money and the easiest workloads are, creating a situation where caregiver teams are constantly being fractured.

When asked about her own views towards excellent patient care, Mary Essary is inspiring. "I could never *not* be a nurse," she assures me.[14] When it comes to attending a dying patient she said:

> I've been with a lot of patients when they left this world. Often it's only them and me. At that point it's

not so much about giving them hope as it is rein-
forcing a belief in them. It's about helping them
believe that God loves them and that it's OK to leave
this world. I can picture the faces of those particular
patients. What I try to do is prevent that terrible
loneliness that would just devastate me. It's a huge
gift to be able to do that with people.[15]

It is hard to imagine nurses handling their burdens without
the conviction that their job is a sacred calling. The work
is too difficult and complex to be handled without passion.
Mary Essary insisted:

It's easy to believe in nursing. If you care enough
about something, you can do tremendous things.
You can do a lot more than you ever thought you
could do.[16]

Rocky Engbarth, a physician's assistant, also sees his role
in the dying process as a gift. For him, excellent care also
means being truthful and preparing the patient emotionally
and spiritually for death. Rocky was unable to say good-bye
properly when his own father died, and he is convinced that
one of the privileges of his job is also helping family members
say good-bye to each other.

Being truthful is a gift to the patient. The more
truthful you are, the more you can help them prepare
themselves for death and say good-bye to their loved
ones.[17]

Rocky also pointed out that he gives patients of all spiritual backgrounds a similar encouragement:

> When I watch people go, I give them the simplest
> comfort I know, which is, "I'll see you down the
> road. Save a place for me."[18]

Being willing to hug and touch patients, express empathy, and pray with patients are other ways to develop the intimacy required for excellent health care. Linda Scheurer reminded me that her patients often come in angry or frustrated. They may blame their caregivers for their illness or they may resent the hastiness of some doctors. Often they're just afraid and lonely and lash out at whoever comes near.[19]

My daughter Laurie frequently prays with her patients. She says she has never been rebuked when proposing a prayer. As I have previously stated in Kasey's story, she pointed her finger at me and said, "You need to pray for all of your patients!" I do pray for many of my patients and always ask for permission when I feel it is appropriate to pray audibly with a patient. When it doesn't feel appropriate to pray audibly, I will frequently pray silently for my patients. None of the nurses I spoke with pray with every patient; they let their instincts guide them. When the patient trusts his nurse, he will more often complain about how the illness is terrifying him, interfering with his hopes and dreams, and affecting his family. Frequently these complaints lead to the discussion of the patient's faith or his doubts about the afterlife. All the nurses I spoke with felt comfortable speaking about their own faith; they viewed this as another privilege of their job. Laurie says she frequently gives hugs or holds a patient's hands. Much of the time that a patient is in the hospital they are in between tests and procedures with nothing to do but think. The healing touch, when offered in moments like these, can be medicine for the soul.

Before I begin the physical examination of a patient, I offer him or her a handshake. If we develop a more intimate relationship, and especially if they are experiencing significant life struggles, I'll give them a hug. Hugs can be therapeutic in the midst of crises, not only for the patient and his or her family but for the caregiver. One illustration of the importance of touching is the way physicians use their stethoscopes. Being a cardiologist, I'm always carrying a stethoscope around my neck. This instrument is only of value when it's connected at both ends. I almost wish I could shorten the stethoscope to bring me closer. Caregivers forget how intimidating and lonely health care facilities can be for the patient. Doctors who are emotionally distant and noticeably in a hurry make the situation even more tense. Handshakes, pats on the back, and simple gestures like smiles and kind words can help humanize the otherwise sterile environment.

These ideas are not new and can be found in Scripture. Proverbs 16:24 reads, "Pleasant words are a honeycomb, sweet to the soul and healing to the bones." Cheerfulness and sincere affection have definite healing value. Proverbs 17:22 reads, "A cheerful heart is good medicine, but a crushed spirit dries up the bones." When there is no immediate medical solution for a patient, when that patient lies with a crushed spirit, I can still try to leave him or her with hope.

As I have realized, God is in charge of life and death. I have learned that God's grace extends throughout our life. His hope is ever present. As we've discussed, and as Dr. Peabody mentioned, one's will to live and general feeling of hope can influence his or her recovery as much as tests and medicine. As Dr. Peabody has pointed out:

> Sickness produces an abnormally sensitive emotional
> state in almost everyone, and in many cases the
> emotional state repercusses, as it were, on the organic
> disease.[20]

I spoke to several hospital administrators in Colorado about the challenges of providing quality care in the midst of financial pressures. I also spoke to them about how they view their role in the caring profession and how their faith influences their job. Administrators oversee an enormous health care budget. They balance the tasks of marketing, buying medicine and equipment, maintaining the safety and integrity of the hospital structure, and much more.

Ruthita Fike and David Crane are hospital administrators who are both personal friends of mine. Both work for nonprofit providers who offer faith-based care as part of their mission statement. I introduced Ruthita earlier. David Crane was the CEO at Littleton Adventist Hospital outside Denver and recently moved to Hinsdale, Illinois, to be the CEO/president of the Midwest Adventist Hospital System. They complained that financial pressures have become more intense in the last 15 years, partly due to the changing nature of health insurance companies. Many people do not realize that most insurance companies initially had nonprofit status. Their mission was to share risk among a large pool of patients. When I spoke to David in December of 2003, he estimated that up to 90 percent of insurance companies are now out for profit. They now avoid risk. Patients with predispositions to diabetes and heart disease are "avoided like the plague."[21] Pure business interests are influencing a profession that both Ruthita and David consider to be a sacred calling. He told me:

I think health care should be faith-based and nonprofit because of the nature of what we do. As a Christian, I see myself as a steward of God's assets. Like the Parable of the Talents [Matt. 25:14–30], I think we have been given a lot of talents here and it is our job to administer and optimize those talents for His service. My job as a CEO is to support 1,100 people in my hospital in that mission of extending themselves as Christ's hands. I see it as a ministry. We have the chance to open the dialogue between patients, their families, and staff about spiritual matters when they're in the middle of a crisis.[22]

People may not expect the administrators to let their faith guide their handling of financial matters, but the two I spoke to made it clear what guides their work. Ruthita told me that she opens almost every meeting among other top-level administrators with prayer. It may surprise people how an industry so heavily dominated by science can be administrated by people whose spirituality is not only fundamental to their work, but also embraced by the majority of their coworkers. Ruthita has sensed condescension towards her faith on only a few occasions, and David has never really felt like the spiritual direction of his leadership has been challenged.[23]

Barb Van Horne shared the story of another instance when she believed God made the difference. Early in Barb's career, a new mother in her twenties named Rebecca was admitted into Barb's care because of a headache.[24] The caregivers believed it was a migraine at first, but the patient quickly became more confused and belligerent, which is atypical of migraines. They transferred Rebecca to another hospital for a CT scan. The physicians determined that she suffered from herpes encephalitis, which was causing her brain to swell. Rebecca eventually slipped into a coma that lasted for the next four months. Her husband stayed by her side, praying, reading, and talking to her; nonetheless, she gave no response. Several times, against the odds, her ventilator became disconnected, which would have killed her if her husband had not been by her side.

As the months wore on, the doctors told Rebecca's husband that even if she did wake up, her functioning would be seriously impaired. After four months she was transferred back into Barb's care temporarily before she was to be moved to a hospice. Rebecca required lots of attention. The caregivers fed her through a tube and frequently had to flip her over to prevent bedsores. One day Barb was especially busy and had to reposition the patient without any help. The patient was heavy and difficult to move, and Barb became frustrated. "Rebecca, help me!" Barb cried out. "Would you at least grab the side rail and pull yourself over?"[25] To her surprise, Rebecca responded for the first time in four months and grabbed the side rail. Barb suspected it might have been just a reflex, so she began giving Rebecca further prompts. "Squeeze my hand," Barb said, and the patient responded weakly. Barb called the husband, who was sleeping at home. He didn't seem to believe the story, but came in anyway. Over the next few days, Rebecca became stronger and stronger. She eventually walked out of the hospital, communicating well and on her way to recovery. She had no memory of the previous five months. A month or so after she was discharged, she came back, ecstatic, sharing with Barb that she was menstruating again and could therefore have another child.

Barb believes there are some cases where scientific explanations don't tell the full story. When it comes to Rebecca's success, Barb gives God the credit. When her ventilator became detached, when her husband stayed by her side praying, when Barb asked Rebecca to squeeze her hand, God was again the ultimate advocate.[26]

The willingness of Rebecca's husband to stay by her side during her coma also brings up another important point. The quantity and quality of loving relationships in one's life is perhaps the best predictor of a person's sense of fulfillment and mental health. Dr. Dossey writes:

> If scientists suddenly discovered a drug that was as powerful as love in creating health, it would be heralded as a medical breakthrough and marketed overnight—especially if it had as few side effects and was as inexpensive as love. Love is intimately related with health. That is not a sentimental exaggeration.[27]

Dr. Dossey cites a survey of 10,000 men with heart disease. Those men who perceived their wives as supportive and loving experienced a 50 percent reduction in frequency of chest pain.[28] God often uses the love of key individuals in our lives as a means of extending to us the care He knows we need.

Let's examine what patients can do to improve the quality of care. One way is by being exceptional patients. Dr. Bernie Siegel discusses the importance of being an exceptional patient in his book *Love, Medicine, and Miracles.*[29] Dr. Seigel, who practices pediatric oncology surgery, has observed that aggressive, stubborn patients who don't settle for medical care they aren't satisfied with end up having much better long-term health than more passive patients, who hide the frustration they feel or give in to a mood of hopelessness. Exceptional patients won't accept explanations and answers they aren't satisfied with. We touched on this issue in chapter 3 when describing my previous patient, Kasey. Kasey would get in my face and grill me with questions, constantly seeking further clarification. Siegel cites a study result that tracked a series of cancer victims over a number of years. Patients who responded to their diagnosis with a "fighting spirit" had 10-year survival rates of 75 percent. Patients who responded with "stoic acceptance," or feelings of helplessness and hopelessness, had 10-year survival rates of 22 percent.[30]

Caregivers may not always be in the mood for the extra time and energy that exceptional patients demand, but Dr. Siegel stresses that this stubborn attitude translates to better health. He cites other studies that show that people with "fighting spirit" have higher levels of T-cells (T-Lymphocytes) in their blood, which help fight disease.[31] According to Dr. Siegel:

> People who always smile, never tell anyone their troubles, and neglect their own needs are the ones who are most likely to become ill.[32]

For exceptional patients, the attitude should always be "no" when dealing with uncaring, unclear, and unsatisfactory medical care. Ruthita Fike told me that hospitals are taking proactive measures to help patients be more assertive about their medical rights.[33] There has been a major effort by many hospitals in recent times to educate patients about the role they play in the healing process to make them, in effect, their own advocates. She says, "For financial reasons, patients now undergo a concentrated array of procedures and treatments while they're here. Patients who are fearful are not in a state where they can always process medical advice well."[34] All of the advice and information, Ruthita suggests, can be overwhelming, especially to senior citizens. Doctors are not often as patient as they could be. Efforts to make patients their own advocates teach them to demand clear instructions, even repeated instructions, until the information is understood.

We've seen how various caregivers take turns being patient advocates. Many of the caregivers I spoke to insisted that their work was not just a job but a sacred calling, even a ministry. It is not a ministry in the sense that unwelcome spiritual discussion is forced on patients, but rather because God is the ultimate advocate for patients. When caregivers can help mend a patient's relationship with God, they are enabling that patient to use a lifeline that will never fail them. Even the nurses, who spend eight hours or more a day with a patient, cannot be with the patient always, nor can they ever offer saving grace and eternal love the way God can.

Certainly, not every caregiver has a faith. I spoke to some caregivers who are not comfortable talking about their own faith with patients. But caregivers should not get into the caring profession prepared to remain indifferent to spiritual matters. They will find that direct patient care involves dealing with people who are frequently in a spiritual crisis. These spiritual crises can be more painful and more important to patients than their physical pain. Caregivers have the unique challenge of giving hope to the hopeless during the darkest moments of their life. When a caregiver is indifferent or hostile towards the spiritual crises of patients, he is mismanaging part of his job. Even if caregivers cannot give hope directly, they should sense when a patient wants spiritual guidance and seek the counsel of the hospital chaplain or the patient's family, friends, pastor, rabbi, or priest.

It is also worth mentioning again that God works through people regardless of their faith, even when they are not aware of it. Once I was referring a Christian patient to a heart surgeon I respected who happened to be Jewish. The patient inquired about the surgeon's faith, and when I told him, the patient responded that he wanted only a Christian physician. I responded that I had seen God work through this physician many times, and I felt he was the best man for the job. If we realize that God is in control and that God is the one who does the healing, then we should be confident that God will work with whomever He chooses. This is one of the reasons I pray for the caregiver as well as the patient.

It is worthwhile to realize how God's Holy Spirit works in our lives, especially when we are confronted by illness. The Holy Spirit, as we've mentioned before, is one person of the Trinity. We are chosen by God the Father, we have belief in Christ the Son, while the Holy Spirit serves as God's seal. The Spirit demonstrates that we belong to Him, that He will keep His promises to us, that we are new creations by His grace. This Spirit dwells in our heart, comforts us, prays for us, and convicts when we stray from God's plan for us. As it says in Romans 8:26:

> The Spirit helps us in our weakness. We do not know what we ought to pray for, but the Spirit intercedes for us with groans that words cannot express.

This Holy Spirit, the very presence of God, is our ultimate advocate and our strongest advocate. God promises that He will never leave us or forsake us. (See Deuteronomy 31:6.)

Linda Scheurer told me that she has observed that most patients who have made miraculous recoveries had a personal relationship with this Holy Spirit. She has noticed that such patients remain determined to beat their illness but no longer fear death.[35] They develop an attitude of acceptance, trusting that God will be with them in life or in death.

At my death I believe there will be a reunion with my Savior. As we've mentioned before, our ultimate healing is a healing of our soul. Physical healing may not happen in this life, but through Christ it will happen in the life to come. When I die and come before the throne of grace, I know that Jesus will be beside me, just as He was beside me when Steve, from chapter 4, looked up from his hospital bed and saw Jesus standing by my right side. This gives me tremendous encouragement. When I meet God, our Father, I believe I will be asked, "What brings you here? What gives you the right of salvation?" I will answer that nothing I have done has justified me. It's all about who I am with and what He has done for me. Jesus has promised to be my caring advocate, my shepherd, my counselor, my redeemer, and my savior. My salvation is not about me. It is all about being touched and transformed by His grace through faith in Jesus. May God's grace also touch and transform you.

NOTES

Chapter 1—Touched by God's Grace

1.   George W. Bush, "Why History Is Important," speech given September 17, 2002, transcript accessed at George Mason University's History News Network, http://www.hnn.us/articles/980.html (January 7, 2010).

2.   George W. Bush, "Bush Speaks on Strengthening Social Security," speech given April 9, 2002, transcript accessed at CNN.com, http://transcripts.cnn.com/TRANSCRIPTS/0204/09/se.02.html (January 7, 2010).

3.   James Shedlock, "Review of Osler's 'A Way of Life' and Other Addresses...," *Journal of the Medical Library Association* 90:3 (July 2002), http://www.ncbi.nlm.nih.gov/pmc/articles/PMC116415/ (accessed January 7, 2010).

4.   Bernie Siegel, MD, *Love, Medicine, and Miracles* (New York City: Harper Collins, 1986), 14.

5.   Linda Sheehan, personal interview, March 2004.

6.   Félix Martí-Ibañez, MD, *To Be a Doctor* (New York City: MD Publications, 1968), 7.

7.   Ibid., 10.

8.   E. M. Bounds, *Power Through Prayer* (Grand Rapids, MI: Baker Book House, 1993), 11.

9.   Ibid.

Chapter 2—Prayer: Dependent Humility Before God

1.   Peter Kreeft quote accessed at www.QuoteCatholic.com/index/php/tag/peter-kreeft, February 8, 2010.

2.   Mother Teresa, *Everything Starts with Prayer* (Ashland, OR: White Cloud Press, 1998), 15.

3.   Carol Osman Brown quote accessed at www.Finestquotes.com (January 12, 2010).

4.   *Life Application Bible Study Bible: New International Version* (Wheaton, IL: Tyndale House, 1985), 2083.

5. Rev. Setan Lee, personal interview, April 6, 2002. Also, Rev. Setan Lee, e-mail to the author, February 1, 2010.

6. Bud Sparling, personal interview, January 2003.

7. Mother Teresa, *Everything Starts with Prayer*, 41.

8. Dr. Don Sweeting, personal interview, July 2003.

9. Dr. Jim Dixon, personal interview, May 2003.

10. E. M. Bounds, *Power Through Prayer*, 14.

11. Bob Beltz, MD, *Transforming Your Prayer Life* (Brentwood, TN: Wodgemuth and Hyatt, 1991), 47.

12. Dr. Sweeting, interview.

13. Sparling, interview.

14. Dr. Sweeting, interview.

15. Ibid.

16. Linda Williams, personal interview, March 2008.

17. Thomas Newman, MD, "Approaching Prayer in the Medical Setting," *The Journal of Christian Healing* Vol. 22, No. 1 and 2 (Spring/Summer 2000): 35–43.

18. Thomas Newman, MD, personal interview, March 2008.

19. Ibid.

20. Ibid.

21. Ibid.

22. Dr. Dixon, interview.

23. Dr. Sweeting, interview.

24. Ibid.

25. Dr. Dixon, interview.

26. C. S. Lewis, *Mere Christianity* (New York City: Scribner, 1942), 176–177.

27. Dr. Sweeting, interview.

CHAPTER 3—KASEY'S STORY: A NEAR-DEATH VISION OF THE CITY OF GOD

1. Kasey, testimony given at Calvary Hill Church.

2. Kasey, personal interview, 1991.

3. Ibid.

4. Dr. Sweeting, interview.

5. Siegel, *Love, Medicine, and Miracles,* 172, 25.

CHAPTER 4—STEVE'S STORY: REJECTED BY GOD, THEN PEACE WITH GOD

1. Maurice Rawlings, MD, *Beyond Death's Door* (Nashville, TN: Bantam Books, 1978), xi.
2. Ibid., 3–4.
3. Maurice Rawlings, MD, *To Hell and Back* (Nashville, TN: Thomas Nelson, 1993), 36.

CHAPTER 5—HOLY GROUND: THE ROOM OF THE DYING PATIENT

1. Philip Yancey, *Where Is God When it Hurts?* (Grand Rapids, MI: Zondervan, 1990), 73.
2. Dr. Elizabeth Kubler-Ross, *On Death and Dying* (New York City: Touchstone Books, 1969).
3. Ibid., 92.
4. Ibid., 124.
5. Ibid., 21–22.
6. Ibid., 49.
7. Ibid.
8. Ibid.
9. Ibid., 149.
10. Ibid., 151.
11. Karyl, personal interview, March 2003.
12. Ibid.
13. Ibid.
14. Ibid.
15. Diane, personal interview, June 2003.
16. Ibid.
17. Ibid.
18. Chuck, personal interview, June 2003.
19. Ibid.
20. Ibid
21. Ibid.
22. Ibid.
23. Rev. Setan Lee, personal interview, July 2003.
24. William F. Buckley Jr., *A Hymnal* (New York City: G.P. Putnam's Sons, 1975).
25. Rev. Lee, interview.
26. Ibid.

27. Ibid.
28. Ibid.
29. Yancey, *Where Is God When It Hurts?* 145.
30. Ibid.
31. Dr. David Martyn Lloyd-Jones, "Developing a Kingdom Mindset," *The Life and Teachings of Jesus* (OK: New Forest), chapter 9.3.
32. Ibid.
33. Dr. Jim Dixon, *The Sermons on the Mount: The Beatitudes* Vol. 1 (Highlands Ranch, CO: Grace Blvd. Records).
34. Yancey, *Where Is God When It Hurts?* 145.
35. Sister Monika Hellwig, "Good News to the Poor: Do They Understand it Better?" *Tracing the Spirit: Communities, Social Action, and Theological Reflection* (Ramsey, NJ: Paulist Press, 1983), 128.
36. Rev. Brian Myers, sermon delivered at Dillon Community Church, Dillon, Colorado, 2006.
37. Ibid.

CHAPTER 6—DIVINE EXPERIENCES: VISIONS AND VISITATIONS FROM GOD

1. Merl, personal interview, September 2003.
2. Ibid.
3. Ibid.
4. "Notes for Matthew 11:28–30," *The NIV Study Bible* (Grand Rapids, MI: Zondervan, 1985).
5. Bob, personal interview, October 2003.
6. Ibid.
7. Joel Rosenberg, *Inside the Revolution* (Carol Stream, IL: Tyndale House, 2009).
8. Ibid., 384–385.
9. Ibid., 385.
10. Ibid., 384.
11. Ibid., 387.
12. Ibid., 387–388.
13. Ibid., 387.
14. Doug Groothuis, *Deceived by the Light* (Eugene, OR: Harvest House, 1995), 31–32.

CHAPTER 7—FAITH IN SOCIETY: THE CONFLICT BETWEEN THE
PRIDE OF LEARNING AND DEPENDENT HUMILITY BEFORE GOD

1.   Toni R. Young-Huber, RN, personal letter to Dr. Sheehan
thanking him for the care of her father, October 18, 1996.

2.   E and P Staff, "Polls Find Americans Belief in God Remains
Strong," *Saviorquest,* Gallup Survey, December 2005, http://www.
saviorquest.com/news2/pollgod.htm (accessed January 13, 2010).

3.   Gallup Poll, *The New York Times,* September 12, 1976, and
December 31, 1976.

4.   'Ninety-Five Percent of Americans Believe in God,"
UnexplainedStuff.com. http://www.unexplainedstuff.com/Religious-
Phenomena/Ninety-Five-Percent-of-Americans-Believe-in-God.html
(accessed September 2009).

5.   Sean Alfano, "Poll: Majority Belief in Ghosts," *CBS
News,* http://www.cbsnews.com/stories/2005/10/29/opinion/polls/
main994766.shtml (accessed February 8, 2010).

6.   Grant R. Jeffrey, "Search for Immortality," Grant R. Jeffrey
Ministries, www.GrantJeffrey.com.

7.   Survey, Porter Memorial 11th Winter Cardiac Symposium,
1993.

8.   Rawlings, *Beyond Death's Door,* 78.

9.   Todd Maugans, et al., "Religion and Family Medicine: A
Survey of Physicians and Patients," *Journal of Family Practice* Vol.
32 (February 91): 210.

10.   Dr. Carolyn Sorenson, *Survey of Medical Students at
University of Colorado Health Sciences Center,* April 1998.

11.   Susan Mitchell, *American Attitudes,* General Social Survey,
National Opinion Research Center, University of Chicago (Ithaca,
NY: New Strategist Publications, Inc., 2000), 284

12.   American Psychiatric Association, "Task Force on Religion
and Psychiatry," *DSM-IV Sourcebook* Vol. 3 (Washington, DC),
1008.

13.   Ibid.

14.   Peter Gay, ed., *The Freud Reader* (New York: WW Norton
and Company, 1989), 435.

15.   Ibid., 708.

16.   Albert Ellis, "Psychotherapy and Atheistic Values: A
Response to A. E. Bergin's 'Psychotherapy and religious values,'"
Journal of Consulting and Clinical Psychology (1980): 48, 635–639.

17. Frederick Crews, "The Memory Wars: Freud's Legacy in Dispute," *New York Review Of Books* (1995): 8.

18. Peter Medawar, "From Freud and Conflict and Culture," *New York Review of Books,* January 23, 1975, 4.

19. Kevin MacDonald, "Freud's Follies," *Skeptic,* Vol. 4, No. 3, 1996.

20. William R. Breakey, "Psychiatry, Spirituality, and Religion," *International Review of Psychiatry* Vol. 13, No. 2 (May 2001): 61.

21. Michele A. Vu, "Survey: One in Three Scientists Believe in God," *The Christian Post* July 16, 2009, www.christianpost.com/article/20090716 (accessed January 13, 2010).

22. Lee Strobel, *The Case for a Creator* (Grand Rapids, MI: Zondervan, 2004), 65.

23. Ibid., 46.

24. Ibid., 205.

25. Ralph Waldo Emerson quote accessed at BrainyQuote.com.

26. Carl Sandburg, *Abraham Lincoln. The War Years* Vol. 5 (New York City: Harcourt, Brace and Company, 1939), 224.

27. Mitchell, *American Attitudes,* 284.

28. Dr. Larry Dossey, *Healing Words* (New York City: Harper Collins, 1993), 2.

29. Dr. Randolph Byrd, "Positive Therapeutic Effects of Intercessory Prayer in a Coronary Unit Production," *Southern Medical Journal* 81 (1988): 826–829.

30. Dr. Rogerio Lobo, Dr. Kwang Y Cha, Daniel P. Wirth, JD, MS, "Does Prayer Influence the Success of in Vitro Fertilization–Embryo Transfer?" *Journal of Reproductive Medicine* Vol. 46 (2001): 781–787.

31. Leonard Leibovici, "Effects of Remote, Retroactive Intercessory Prayer on Outcomes in Patients with Bloodstream Infection," British Medical Journal Vol. 323, Issue 7327 (December 22, 2001): 1450.

32. Dossey, *Healing Words,* 31.

33. Dr. Sweeting, interview.

34. "Americans Who Give Up Religion," *Journal for the Scientific Study of Religion* Vol. 76, No. 2138: 144.

35. Dale A Matthews, *The Faith Factor* (New York City: Penguin Books, 1998), 135.

36. Dr. J. S. Levin, "Religion and Health: Is There an Association, Is It Valid, and Is It Causal?" *Social Science and Medicine* (1994): 1475–1482.
37. Ibid.
38. Dianne Hales, "Why Prayer Could Be Good Medicine," *Parade,* March 23, 2003, 4.
39. E. M. Bounds, *Power Through Prayer.*

CHAPTER 8—THE CARING AND HEALING PROFESSION: OUR ULTIMATE ADVOCATE

1. Dr. A. McGehee Harvey, et al., "The Approach of the Patient," *The Principles and Practice of Medicine, 18th ed.* (New York City: Appleton-Century-Crofts, 1972), 1.
2. Francis Weld Peabody, MD, "The Care of the Patient," *Journal of the American Medical Association* Vol. 88, No. 12 (March 19, 1927): 877–882, quoted in Dr. A. McGehee Harvey, et al., *The Principles and Practice of Medicine, 18th ed.,* 1.
3. Paul Oglesby and the Francis S. Countway Library of Medicine in cooperation with the Harvard Medical Association, "The Caring Physician: The Life of Dr. Francis W. Peabody" (Boston, MA: The Harvard University Press, 1991).
4. Francis Weld Peabody, MD, "The Care of the Patient."
5. Dr. Peter V. Tishler, *Paros Alpha Omega Alpha Honor Medical Society* Vol. 55, No. 3 (Summer 1992): 37.
6. Mark W. Sheehan, MD, "Diagnostic Errors in Clinical Practice," *Texas Medicine* Vol. 74 (1978): 92–100.
7. Ibid.
8. Ruthita Fike, personal interview, December 2002.
9. Mary Essary, personal interview, November 2003.
10. Mary Soltau, personal interview.
11. Linda Scheurer, personal interview, November 2003.
12. Essary, interview.
13. Ibid.
14. Ibid.
15. Ibid.
16. Ibid.
17. Rocky Engbarth, personal interview, October 2003.
18. Ibid.
19. Scheurer, interview.

20. Francis Weld Peabody, MD, "The Care of the Patient."
21. David Crane, personal interview, October 2003.
22. Ibid.
23. Crane, interview; and Fike, interview.
24. Barb Van Horne, personal interview, February 2004.
25. Ibid.
26. Ibid.
27. Dossey, *Healing Words*, 109.
28. Ibid.
29. Dr. Siegel, *Love, Medicine, and Miracles.*
30. Ibid., 25.
31. Ibid.
32. Ibid., 172.
33. Fike, interview.
34. Ibid.
35. Scheurer, interview.

TO CONTACT THE AUTHOR

www.hpohg.com

Mark W. Sheehan, MD: msheehan@hpohg.com

Chris Sheehan: csheehan@hpohg.com